■SCHOLA

The Primary
Teacher's Guide to
History

Key subject knowledge • Background information • Teaching tips •

Paul Noble

■ SCHOLASTIC

Book End, Range Road, Witney, Oxfordshire, OX29 0YD
www.scholastic.co.uk
© 2012 Scholastic Ltd
23456789 2345678901

British Library Cataloguing-in-Publication Data
A catalogue record for this book is available from the
British Library.

ISBN 978-1407-12782-8
Printed and bound by CPI Group (UK) Ltd, Croydon,
CR0 4YY.

Author
Paul Noble

Commissioning Editor
Paul Naish

Development Editor
Pollyanna Poulter

Proofreader
Kate Manson

Indexer
Penny Brown

Illustration
Garry Davies

Icons
Tomek.gr

Series Designers
Shelley Best and Sarah Garbett

Acknowledgements
Every effort has been made to trace copyright
holders for the works reproduced in this book,
and the publishers apologise for any inadvertent
omissions.

About the author
Paul Noble's teaching career began in London but
he went on to become a primary headteacher and
history adviser in Wiltshire. He has been involved in
supporting history teaching through the Historical
Association and English Heritage and has written
many books for teachers and children.

Contents

	Introduction	5
Chapter 1	Starting history topics	8
Chapter 2	The Great Fire of London	20
Chapter 3	Ancient Egypt	32
Chapter 4	The Ancient Greeks	53
Chapter 5	The Romans	77
Chapter 6	The Anglo-Saxons	94
Chapter 7	The Vikings in Britain	115
Chapter 8	The Aztecs	134
Chapter 9	The Tudors	154
Chapter 10	The Victorians	179
Chapter 11	Britain since 1930	204
Chapter 12	Local history study	228
	Glossary	238
	Index	244

Icon key

Information within this book is highlighted in the margins by a series of different icons. They are:

Subject facts
Key subject knowledge is clearly presented and explained in this section.

Why you need to know these facts
Provides justification for understanding the facts that have been explained in the previous section.

Common misconceptions
Identifies and corrects some of the common misconceptions and beliefs that may be held about the subject area.

Vocabulary
A list of key words, terms and language relevant to the preceding section. Vocabulary entries appear in the glossary.

Amazing facts
Interesting snippets of background knowledge to share.

Teaching ideas
Outlines practical teaching suggestions using the knowledge explained in the preceding section.

Handy tips
Specific tips or guidance on best practice in the classroom.

Sensitive issues
Highlights areas that require consideration before presentation to the class, including personal, social and cultural issues.

History

History is a story that cannot be told without one vital ingredient: the fact. Although we could debate long and hard as to what constitutes an historical fact (historians do), the need for information in order to communicate the past to children is indisputable. One Ofsted report, in 2011, asserted that 'primary history lacked an over-arching narrative because teachers did not know enough'. Teachers need facts. Teachers cannot know everything, and it would be ridiculously unreasonable to expect them to; however, they must know some history.

This *Teacher's Guide* aims to help out in this area by summarising some basic information that will help teachers in Key Stage 1 and Key Stage 2 to teach the subject.

History remains a 'foundation' subject and it is an important one, even though its uses are not obviously utilitarian. If children are to understand the world around them, and indeed their place within it, they will need to acquire some knowledge of the past. They ought to learn about castles and cathedrals and kings and queens, but mostly they ought to learn about people, about the successive waves of migrations and immigrations that have affected these islands and about the lives of individuals, both ordinary and extraordinary, within them. It is up to teachers to tell a good story.

Popular and enduring topics have been selected for this book. For example, in Chapters 1 and 2 you will find examples of possible KS1 infant study topics, together with the sorts of questions that might be asked in order to bring a proper historical focus to these studies. With older infants, when the curriculum may take on a more discrete historical character, you may choose to study some famous individuals in history. This book directs you to particular people within a chosen event (for example, Samuel Pepys' involvement with the Great Fire

Introduction

of London, see pages 28–9), but you may also examine likely KS2 topics to find suitable historical characters to study. For example, Florence Nightingale links with Victorian Britain (see pages 197–8); Alfred the Great links with Anglo-Saxon Britain and the Danish invasions (see page 111). You might also look for historical figures in your locality, as this provides a young child with a connection to their known world. Statues are a good starting point. There is one of I. K. Brunel not far from where I sit; it provides local schools with an opportunity not to be missed.

For KS2, popular and enduring topics have again been selected. An overview of 'Invaders' is given at the start of the chapter on the Romans. Whichever group of invaders you choose to study, you will need to locate them within the context of the whole series of invasions and settlements that took place in Britain during the first millennium and beyond. Indeed, whatever topic you are studying with your children you will need to place the events in the context of time and place. Introduce them to dates and the language of time. Help them to know and understand events, their causes and outcomes. Teach them about the nature and value of evidence. Above all, good history teaching requires a focus upon people and the telling of stories that will grip the children's imagination.

The study of history is fascinating mainly because it is about people, and nothing interests us more than ourselves. However, history is not about learning everything about the past, for the past is huge and ultimately unknowable and we can only create our own partial view of it based upon evidence. So do not expect to be able to teach your children everything about the Romans or the Victorians – this cannot be done. Similarly, this book cannot include all the information that is known about these topics – we have made a careful selection of what to cover, just as you must do. Remember, focus on people and tell stories that will grip the children's imaginations, because ultimately it is with our imaginations that we really comprehend truth.

Need to know more?

Facts

Those interested in the nature of history and the debate over what constitutes a historical fact could consult the short book by E. H. Carr, *What is History?* (Palgrave Macmillan, 2002), first published over 40 years ago and now available with a new introduction by Richard J. Evans. For a detailed academic examination of the historian's art you might move on to the more controversial *The New Nature of History: Knowledge, Evidence, Language* by the late Arthur Marwick (Palgrave Macmillan, 2001).

The National Curriculum

It hardly needs stating that the government's education website is the place to go for up-to-date information and publication lists: **www.education.gov.uk/schools**

Due to the periodic modification that affects the National Curriculum, publications on its nature tend to date rather quickly. For a cogent, well-written book that is not wedded to National Curriculum structure but examines general issues relating to the teaching of the subject, the enthusiastic Prof. Chris Husbands' book, *What is History Teaching?* (Open University Press, 1996), is a thoughtful read. *Teaching History 3–11* by O'Hara and O'Hara (Continuum, 2001) does not have the same literary merit and will not set your pulse racing, but does cover all the bases, from gender issues to planning.

A note on resources

It is clearly impossible to list every useful museum, book or website on the topics in this book; the lists would effectively be endless. But key references are given in the resources sections at the end of each chapter. These are enough to work with, but also provide good starting points for those who want to investigate further.

Chapter 1

Starting history topics

Young primary school children are at a very early stage on the path to historical understanding. They are only just starting to explore the past and lay the foundations for future learning and understanding. Facts, dates and judgments – the very stuff of academic history – are therefore comparatively unimportant when it comes to teaching history to them.

Before they can do anything else, young children need to understand that the past exists, that it is big, and that it is separate from the present. In Reception and Year 1, you can lead children towards this understanding and start to provide them with the language and vocabulary to enable them to talk about the past and begin a tentative exploration of it. As a result, the approach in this chapter must be different from that used in the others.

What areas of study?

Children need to acquire historical knowledge, skills and understanding, but they can only do this by studying a topic with clear historical content. Ideally, at the beginning of KS1 they should study a history topic that can be connected to their own personal experience, for example to 'changes in their own lives and the way of life of their family or others around them'. There are many topics fit for this purpose. The topics Holidays and Homes, outlined in this chapter, are good examples, although there are, of course, many other topic themes from which the needs of your history curriculum can be met. For example:

Toys
Shops and shopping

School
Growing up in the past
When teacher (or other suitable adult) was young
People who help us, using a 'then and now' approach, for
    example looking at teachers, shopkeepers, farmers,
    builders or dentists as objects of study
Life on a farm
Great grandpa (or grandma)
Childhood games
Travel
The high street
Keeping the house clean

General topics such as these are well suited to Reception and Year 1. Alternatively, you could choose to study a famous person. Some schools elect to leave this approach to Year 2 when a 'person study' can be linked with the study of a particular historical event. Sometimes the study of a famous person can virtually be thrust upon you, when a name arises naturally from other work or when there is a national commemoration or significant anniversary highlighting the achievements of a particular individual. You can also get ideas from checking what commemorative stamps the Post Office® are scheduled to issue:
www.royalmail.com/personal/stamps-and-collecting
The list of people who might make a suitable subject for study is probably endless so it is a good idea to choose someone who you feel enthusiastic about. Enthusiasm is catching. Try to illustrate the difference between now and then, and demonstrate how things change over time. Here are a few widely differing suggestions:

Amy Johnson (pilot and adventurer)
Mary Seacole (Victorian Scottish-Jamaican nurse)
Queen Elizabeth II (British monarch)
Scott of the Antarctic (explorer)
Roald Dahl (fighter pilot, children's author)
Sir Robert Baden-Powell (founder of the Scout group)
Henry Fox Talbot (photographer)
Margaret Hookham (Dame Margot Fonteyn, ballerina)
Charlie Chaplin (comic, mime artist, actor, film director)

Check local sources for ideas. Historical topics due to be studied at a later date are worth trawling for suitable subjects. From the period of the Great Fire of London, you could study Samuel Pepys, Sir Christopher Wren or Charles II. Look at the topics for KS2: each has key figures worthy of study, although bear in mind the age of your children and look for strong storylines that will appeal to them. You might consider Florence Nightingale or David Livingstone alongside Victorian studies; Hereward the Wake in Anglo-Saxon studies; or Queen Elizabeth I in Tudor studies.

Approaching the subject facts

How you bring the subject facts to the children's attention is more important than the facts themselves. Select a simple question and then set out to answer it. (This approach can be continued for any historical study – at KS2 the children can come up with their own questions to which they wish to find answers.)

The broader the question, the more complex the answer: compare 'What were holidays like in the past?' with 'What was it like to go on holiday when grandma was a child?' The latter is a better question for young children to tackle: it is more precise, more manageable and more understandable.

Holidays

Subject facts

A sensible starting point is the child's own experience of a holiday, making it a good topic with which to start a new school year. You will need to build up strong images of the children's holidays and a bank of pictures, objects and stories to use for comparative work.

Choose also a period in the past for comparison. Children do not have a precise vocabulary for measuring time so there is no need to be pedantic about this. You may opt to use holiday experiences from a number of different decades; within living memory is best although, given sufficient resources, you could focus on the Edwardian or late Victorian period.

Keep the project focus simple, using the 'question' approach mentioned on the previous page. For example:

How did people (for example, grandma) travel?
How did they enjoy themselves?
Where did they go?
What accommodation did they stay in?
How long did they stay?
What did they wear on the beach?
Did they use suntan lotion?
What is the same/different between then and now?

If you choose, for example, the 1950s as the period of comparison, you will need to establish in your own mind the historical context and learn a few relevant facts.

The seaside in the 1950s

Children in the 1950s were mostly experiencing the seaside and holidays for the first time. As with bananas and white bread, they had been denied this pleasure during wartime. The war was still very close in people's memories. Meteor jet fighters of the RAF routinely 'buzzed' the holiday beaches as a way of showing the flag and boosting civilian morale, which in spite of the end of the war was still quite low. Some wartime restrictions, such as rationing, lingered on, however during the 1950s the country began to enter a period of high employment and growing affluence. Harold Macmillan's famous 'You've never had it so good' speech was made in 1959. Between 1951 and 1955 wages rose by 20 per cent in real terms and one of the first priorities for people spending this money was holidays.

Bank holidays marked a big exodus from the cities, even more than they do today. Massive traffic jams occurred at places like the Exeter bypass and on the way to the Lake District. Special coach and rail excursions were provided to cater for the trip to the seaside.

On arriving at the seaside, holiday-makers often found decaying and neglected promenades and piers – little had changed since the Edwardian era. The detritus of war was still visible in the early 1950s, especially along the eastern and southern coasts, and children would often clamber over abandoned gun emplacements without any real knowledge

of what they were.
Fairgrounds contained
rifle ranges, coconut shies
and 'What the butler saw'
peep-shows, mostly of
pre-war origin. The ladies
undressing in the latter
were usually Edwardian.
(I know – I saw 'What
the butler saw!') Fish
and chip lunches, whelks
and cockles, end-of-pier
concerts, a look through
a penny telescope, ice
cream, sticks of rock,
candy floss and Punch
and Judy shows were the
main attractions. Walking

along the promenade was popular with the older generation,
perhaps also visiting the town gardens or a waxwork display, or
listening to a band concert. The package holiday industry had not
developed and many people stayed in cheap lodgings, caravans or
chalets, or on camp sites.

Why you need to know these facts

Young children need to learn that the past is different from the
present, and should have opportunities to ask questions about
the information given to them about the past.

Amazing facts

In 1955, the average weekly wage was £11 7s 10d (£11.39p in
decimal money – equivalent to around £200 in today's money).
Although people were able to find money for a holiday, they
rarely went abroad.

Teaching ideas

● Tell the Punch and Judy story. Make or play with puppets (or both).
● Make a list of all the games that you might play on the beach today. Compare them with the chosen period. What did people do in past times?
● Picture displays can be used to illustrate the ways in which people travel to their holiday destinations. Use 'then and now' comparisons.
● Invite an elderly person to come in and describe a journey to the seaside when he or she was little.
● Make a list of all the things sold on a beach. Use 'then and now' comparisons.
● Have a dressing-up session. What clothes do/did children wear to go on holiday? Dressing up can be done on a dummy or mock-up picture on the wall. How do the children's clothes compare with, say, the 1950s? (For example, Fair Isle pullovers, scarves, snake buckle belts, National Health spectacles, wool swimsuits.)
● Make a bar chart showing the different ways in which the class travelled to their holiday destinations. Compare this with great-grandpa's time.
● Use pictures or words to sequence the main events in a journey to a holiday destination for 'then' and 'now'. Ask the children to order and re-order the words or pictures.
● Collect and display holiday memorabilia. Discuss or show 'then and now' differences.
● Make a 'holidays in the past' display. You could start with photographs of adults and then put information about their holiday experiences as a child underneath the picture.
● Links with other subjects and topics are easily made. You might consider looking at: sand and its uses; the qualities of wet and dry sand; the biblical story of the man who built his house upon sand; floating and sinking; pebbles, stones and shells; seashore animals; travel; places on a map; and so on.

Homes

Subject facts

Homes, not houses, are the focus of this topic, so remember to link the work you do to the lives of the people who live or have lived in the buildings that you study. This should be a cross-curricular project well suited to the very youngest children.

Begin by looking at how houses are built – building sites fascinate most children. Try to arrange a visit to one; there will be an opportunity for health and safety work here. Most of the project should be a 'then and now' comparison. It will be more interesting if you choose a particular person or home to study. Sensitivity will be needed if you use this strategy; think before you enquire too deeply.

Use the question approach as before, for example:

What was it like to live in (your grandparents') home?
What did the furniture look like?
What equipment did they use in the kitchen?
How did they amuse themselves at home in the evenings?
Did their house have double glazing, central heating, television?
Does their house still exist?
How has it changed?

Why you need to know these facts

At KS1, the historical focus needs to be on people's lives and lifestyles. Studying homes provides valuable clues to life in the recent past and gives lots of opportunities to compare 'now' and 'then'.

Amazing facts

● 100,000 London homes were destroyed by bombs in World War II.
● People have lived in houses for about 10,000 years. Buildings made of mud bricks (dating from around 8000 years ago) have been discovered at Catal Hoyuk in Turkey. (In Turkish, it is Çatalhöyük, one of three permitted spellings.)
● Bricks used to be made in all sorts of sizes until standard dimensions were established about 100 years ago.

Teaching ideas

● Examine the difference between a house and a home.
● Make a chart of words that describe the homes of different people. (Extending into another subject area, you might like to examine animal homes.)
● Make a bar chart showing the types of homes lived in by children in the class. You could make a comparative chart showing the types of homes lived in by their grandparents. Compare the charts and discuss.
● Look at how a house is made. Invite someone in to talk to the class about building a house.
● Collect poems and stories about houses and homes ('The House that Jack Built', 'The Three Little Pigs').
● Make a photographic display of the homes that the children live in. Be sensitive; it might be best to stick to the exterior of houses for this exercise.
● Make a plan or model on which the children can place a representation of the house, flat, caravan, etc that they live in. In a village this might take the form of a village map.
● Construct a timeline on which you put a named house picture, one for each child, roughly in order of the dates that they were constructed. The children will have to do some detective work at home. (Don't become obsessed with dates, it is sequence that is needed. For example: Tanya's house is older than Jo's; Sam's house is the oldest; Imran lives in a brand new house.)

- Make a display or class book of time-related words (*old, older, before, after* and so on). This might be illustrated in some way to indicate meaning.
- Collect words that describe the buildings that people live in, such as: *house, cottage, bungalow, flat, penthouse, semi-detached, detached, terraced, hut, mansion, chalet* and so on.
- Make an illustrated dictionary of words that describe the different parts of a house (for example, *gutter, rendering, porch, lintel, loft* and so on).
- Focus on one house (say from the 1950s) and try to imagine who lived there in the past. If you have grandparents who used to live there it will help. How did they live? What did their furniture look like? You could do a large wall display of the work.
- Have a 1950s evening. Listen to the wireless, read books, eat snacks or sweets available then, and so on. Dress up in appropriate clothes if possible. You could do similar exercises for an Edwardian home – sing round the piano, sew, knit, read.
- Use a doll's house as the central feature of a study of homes. Name the parts of the house, look at each room in turn, furnish and decorate it. You could start from scratch with a doll's house constructed from boxes and build it up as the project progresses.

Resources

One secret of successful sourcing of history projects for very young children is to know when to stop. If you are not careful you will overwhelm your class with material, and they will not focus on anything sufficiently to make sense of it. So, although there is a list of resources here, be confident that you can select and use a few items to their best advantage.

First there are the objects that the children can bring to the project. For Holidays you should display and use a selection of holiday photographs from family albums – my holiday, mum's holiday when she was a girl, great-grandma's trip to the seaside and so on. Catalogues from travel agents provide useful material, and copies of old travel posters are good for comparative work (old steam railway posters provide particularly useful talking points). Holiday souvenirs are also fun to discuss – always remember that you are looking for 'then and now' comparisons.

You might be lucky to have some old holiday clothes brought in to school. Great-grandpa's knitted swimming trunks, perhaps? One grandparent I know arrived with a motorbike and sidecar to show the vehicle his wife and family used in the 1950s to go on holiday. Whatever gets offered to you, use it – it will have a valuable hands-on quality that is worth a thousand words.

For Homes a 'tinkering table' is ideal, but only put objects on the table that are virtually indestructible or you may be in trouble. Choosing Great-grandma's time for comparison will probably yield the best trawl, although you may be surprised at how few of the ordinary day-to-day objects from that period survive (people only tend to save the precious). For example, would you expect to get for comparison: a 1950s iron; a television; some ceramic ducks; a roll of wallpaper; a 78rpm record; a wooden tennis racket; or an ancient copy of the *Radio Times*? You can only ask and hope. Photographs and pictures are again a vital resource and you should be able to find plenty for the children to examine.

As everything needs to be as 'hands-on' as possible, make sure that you use people as much as you can. An elderly cleaner, retired milkman, great grandpa, or ex-teacher can be a real boon. Select a good volunteer and make the most of him or her. The chief advantage is that the children can interact with the visitor, ask questions and talk. Give the visitor a precise brief but don't arrange a lecture. Let the children set the pace.

Your young children need to be shown that the past existed, so a visit to the park, school or shop that grandma used, or to the now defunct railway station or track, or a session in a relevant museum is important. Alongside this must go pictures – use photographs, films, slides, posters, DVDs and selected images from the internet.

Ideas and teaching strategies

To check on the latest available material you should always peruse the 'usual suspects' online. What can you get from the BBC, TES, Child Education and your favourite publishers? Two Teacher's Guides originally published by English Heritage – *Learning from Objects: A Teacher's Guide* by Gail Durbin et al and *Using Portraits* by Gail Durbin – are the sort of general guides that are particularly useful in suggesting activities of real historical worth. They can be obtained from online booksellers and downloaded as PDF files from the TES website (see page 18).

Websites

www.bbc.co.uk/schools
www.education.scholastic.co.uk/child_education
www.scholastic.co.uk
www.tes.co.uk/teaching-resources
www.vital.ac.uk
www.npg.org.uk/learning/digital/history.php

Books for children

Story and picture books will be among your best resources.
You may find some useful stories amongst your reading scheme
books as well as on the library shelves. New books come along
all the time – they are not always overtly historical but can
provide wonderful and imaginative ways into historical ideas,
especially about the passage of time and the links with past
generations. A few examples are given below:

● *And Miss Carter Wore Pink* by Helen Bradley (Jonathan Cape) –
A touching story of the author's childhood illustrated with her
own paintings to provide a source that can be dipped into.
It focuses on the Edwardian period. Originally published in 1972.
● *Annabel's House* by Norman Messenger (Dorling Kindersley) –
An interactive picture book, containing no text, that has
removeable cutout people. Although this targets the Edwardian
period, it could easily be used for a later period.
● *Beside the Sea* by Roy and Jean Gerrard (Gollancz) – A small
book about past holidays with lovely pictures and rhyming text.
● *From Me to You* by Paul Rogers (Orchard) – A touching story
that links the past to the present through a piece of clothing.
● *Good Girl Granny* by Pat Thomson and Faith Jaques (Gollancz) –
This small and humorous 'reader' is just what you need as
support for a Holidays or Homes topic. Were children really so
good in the past?
● *Granpa* by John Burningham (Puffin) – There are many
books about grandparents and this is one of the most popular.
These stories can be useful when trying to link the past to the
child's experience of the present.
● *Wilfrid Gordon McDonald Partridge* by Mem Fox (Puffin) –
A marvellous story about memories. Wilfrid's search to find out
the meaning of the word 'memory' leads him to question various
elderly people, with some surprising results.

(Although these books are available not all are necessarily in print. You can find them in children's libraries, well-known online booksellers and bookshops. If you need to search for out-of-print books, a good website is **www.abebooks.co.uk**.)

Collecting

Most primary and infant teachers are hoarders and it is a habit worth cultivating, for school purposes at any rate. Look out particularly for picture postcards when you are on holiday or visiting a museum and you can quite quickly build up your own project pack for the history topic you are studying. Small collections of household objects can help to make past-present comparisons a hands-on experience.

Visits

For infant topics such as these, a journey to a special museum is not really recommended unless it is on your doorstep. Small local collections are your best bet. For this age group simply a walk down the high street would be more advisable than a trip to a large museum of national importance. But there are some wonderful collections around the country and it is always worth checking out what resources you might be able to obtain from them, even if it is only some postcards. The National Media Museum in Bradford is excellent (1950s TVs, travel posters, etc): **www.nationalmediamuseum.org.uk**.

There are also some splendid transport museums, including: the Crich Tramway Village in Derbyshire, where you can ride on a tram; the Black Country Living Museum in Dudley; and the Beamish Living Museum in County Durham.

There are a number of first-rate museums of childhood, including: The National Trust Museum of Childhood in Sudbury, Derbyshire (**www.nationaltrust.org.uk/sudburyhall**); the Museum of Childhood in Hackney (**www.museumofchildhood.org.uk**); and the Museum of Childhood in Edinburgh (**www.edinburgh museums.org.uk/Venues/Museum-of-childhood**).

But, as regards visits, perhaps these national treasures are best kept for a more appropriate age and time unless they are on your doorstep.

Chapter 2

The Great Fire of London

The Great Fire of London in 1666 destroyed a huge part of the largely wooden medieval city of London. In doing so, it helped to remove some of the areas that had been breeding grounds for the Great Plague that had decimated the city the year before. As a result of the fire, the city was rebuilt to new standards, although somewhat below the visionary levels proposed by some architects of the time. However, London emerged with a new cathedral, 52 new churches and some healthier, safer housing.

Introducing the Great Fire

Subject facts

Time of day	Event timeline
Midnight	**Sunday 2 September 1666** *The fire begins in a baker's oven at the end of Pudding Lane, not far from the Tower of London.*
3.00am	*Samuel Pepys – eyewitness to the fire and diarist who recorded its events – is woken by a maid at his house in Greenwich, who alerts him to the fire.*
Dawn	*The fire has already destroyed over 300 houses and is still burning.*

Time of day	Event timeline
Midday	Later in the day Pepys reports to King Charles II and the Duke of York and advises that houses in front of the fire should be pulled down to stop it spreading further. Pepys goes to see the Lord Mayor to command him what to do, but finds that the Mayor is exhausted and overwhelmed by the situation. By the afternoon large numbers of people are fleeing by road and river. Attempts to stop the fire are having no effect.
Nightfall	Thinking that his own house might be threatened, Pepys buries some of his belongings and valuables, including his gold, in his garden.

	Monday 3 September
	The Fire is at its peak, fanned by strong winds and helped by the presence of so much combustible material.
	    The Duke of York rides around the city accompanied by his guard to maintain calm.
	    Many country people arrive with carts to help evacuate the population to the surrounding villages.
	    That night St Paul's Cathedral catches fire. Eyewitness accounts report 10,000 houses burning at one time and a smoke cloud an estimated 90km (56 miles) in length.

4.00pm	**Tuesday 4 September** Molten lead from St Paul's roof is running down the street. The Old Bailey and Newgate Prison burn. Late in the day, the wind begins to abate. Houses are blown up to clear the ground in front of the fire.
	Wednesday 5 September The King orders food supplies to be brought in to feed the homeless. More men are brought in to blow up houses in the path of the fire. The fire begins to come under control. Over 200,000 refugees are camped in the fields of Highgate and Islington.
	Thursday 6 September The fire still burns, but less fiercely.
	Friday 7 September Samuel Pepys gets up in the morning and finds that the fire is out.
	The heat of the ashes can still be felt months later.

Why do we need to know about the Great Fire?

Very young children do not need to know every small detail about the event, but some vivid description will help the event to come alive. Many very young children will be unable to cope with four-figure numbers so the use of numerical dating will not mean very much. Children should come to understand:

● the main events of the fire
● significant figures involved in the event (Samuel Pepys, King Charles II, the Mayor of London)
● why the fire started, how it spread, how it was put out
● the effects of the fire upon people and property
● that the fire happened a long time ago (the event could be placed in relation to other events in history, for example after the Romans, and before trains were invented)
● how we know about the fire through the words of people living at the time.

The story of the Great Fire of London

This topic is appropriate for Year 2 children who love stories. It is best to tell it rather than read it, but the following outline could be expanded or modified to suit your taste and needs. The facts are all true.

> A long time ago, a **very** long time ago.
> Long before you were born, there was a fire.
>
> It was no ordinary fire.
>
> This was a giant monster of a fire, one that ate everything in its way – houses, churches, even the tall steeple of a great cathedral reaching up into the sky. This fire devoured them all. Nothing was safe from it.
>
> It began like this.
>
> Thomas Faryner was a hard-working baker. He had been baking bread all day and was feeling very hot. His oven was hot, his bakery was hot, and the streets outside the

bakery were also hot. There had been no rain for weeks. The thatched roofs of the wooden houses were crisp and dry, and the narrow streets of London were sun-baked and dusty.

This all made Thomas feel extra weary and he was really looking forward to going to bed. He quickly raked out the fire in the bread oven, and went upstairs.

He did not sleep for long as he was woken by shouting.

'Fire! Fire!' He quickly jumped out of bed but found that choking smoke blocked the stairs. As fast as he could he looked for another way to escape. Together with his wife and a servant, he climbed out through the bedroom window and onto the roof. 'Help!' they shouted, as loudly as they could.

Soon all the neighbours were out in the street and they were able to climb across the rooftops to safety. Sadly, that was the end of the bakery – but it was just the beginning of the Great Fire.

Later in the night someone woke the Mayor of London and told him that a large part of London was on fire. He looked out of his bedroom window. 'Tish! A woman could put it out!' he said, and went back to bed.

At three o'clock in the morning a servant woke Samuel Pepys, an important man who worked for the king. He thought that the fire was too far off to worry about, and he too went back to bed.

But the next morning Samuel Pepys decided to walk to the city to have a closer look. He found that the fire had already destroyed hundreds of houses and was burning more fiercely every minute. A wind was blowing strongly, and the flames were roaring, like a dragon's breath, leaping from house to house and devouring everything.

Samuel Pepys immediately went to see the king and told him to pull down the houses in front of the fire so that the dragon would have nothing to feed on and would die. King Charles II commanded this to be done.

Pepys then went to see the mayor to give him the king's orders, but by this time the mayor was a frightened man. He had been trying hard to fight the fire and was exhausted. There were tears in his eyes.

'What can I do? What can I do?' he cried.

The fire burned all day Sunday and Monday and on into Tuesday. Thousands of people fled from their homes, trying to carry all their precious possessions with them. Some escaped down the River Thames in boats and barges. Furniture and clothes that these people had to leave behind floated in the river.

Pepys again went to report to the king. The rich people did not want to have their houses pulled down and were holding up the battle against the monster fire. The poor would not leave their houses until the flames actually caught hold. Even the pigeons did not want to leave. Some birds stayed too long, and as they flew up to escape the flames, their wings were singed so they could not fly, and they plummeted to their deaths below.

Pepys told the king that more men were needed to pull the houses down more quickly. So workers were brought from the dockyards and soldiers came to help fight the fire with a new weapon – gunpowder. Soon the air was filled with loud explosions. Boom! Bang! Crash! Some people panicked. They thought that they could hear cannons and that London was being attacked.

But houses were being blown up before the fire could eat them and so, as the wind began to drop, the fight against the fire began to be won.

But it was not quite over. Newgate Prison caught fire. So did the law courts and, worst of all, so did the great cathedral of St Paul's. The metal on its roof melted with the heat and the hot metal ran down the streets like water. The ground near the fire was too hot to walk on and smoke covered the Sun.

By Friday it was clear that the Great Fire of London was out, although firefighters went round with buckets of water putting out the burning embers for days afterwards. And for a long time there was a strange glow in the sky as the ash cloud was blown high over London.

The fire taught a number of lessons. People learned to build houses that were made of brick and that would not burn easily. And Thomas Faryner learned that when you put out a fire, no matter how tired you are, you must make sure that you put it out properly. Otherwise...

How do we know about the Great Fire?

Most of the evidence is documentary. There are many letters, maps, diaries and plans relating to the fire and to the rebuilding of London. Samuel Pepys and John Evelyn kept diaries, but many other people also wrote about the event including, William Burnett (later Bishop of Salisbury), the Earl of Clarendon, William Denton (one of the king's doctors) and William Taswell (a schoolboy at the time). The *London Gazette* gave the official account and there are some splendidly detailed maps from the period which show the extent of the fire. Documents and accounts of the planning and building works after the fire can also be consulted. In the Museum of London, the hoses, helmets and buckets used by the firefighters can be seen. St Paul's Cathedral is also, in a way, evidence of the fire. Designed by Sir Christopher Wren, it was built to replace the medieval cathedral, which was destroyed in the conflagration. He also designed 51 new churches for the burned-out city.

What happened after the fire?

The cost to property was enormous. Out of London's 109 churches, 87 were destroyed. It consumed 151 hectares (373 acres) within the walls of the City of London, and some 13,200 houses. The total cost was estimated at £10 million (London's annual income was £12,000 at the time).
One huge loss was in books and paper as all the warehouses and booksellers were destroyed near St Paul's, as were the many books that had been stored in the cathedral for safety. Their estimated value was £2 million.

Thomas Faryner, the baker in Pudding Lane where the fire started, claimed that he had raked out his oven fires and that the fire had definitely been started on purpose. Although during the fire it was believed that it was started deliberately (by the Dutch or the French), an inquiry afterwards found that the cause was accidental.

Many plans were put forward for the rebuilding of the City of London but none was adopted. The Rebuilding Act of 1667 decreed that the city should be rebuilt upon the old street plan. However, great care was taken to use less combustible materials such as brick and stone, and the new buildings made London a safer and healthier place. The Act also laid down strict rules about how buildings should be constructed.

A monument, designed by Sir Christopher Wren and completed in 1677, was erected close to the site of the start of the fire. It still stands and is open to the public.

Why you need to know these facts

Young children need to be taught about a significant event from the past. The choice of the Great Fire of London is an appropriate one because it was an important and vivid event commemorated by a famous memorial. Because it is an exciting story it can be understood at a simple level and will appeal to young children. It provides ample opportunity for developing the kind of knowledge, skills and understanding that the teaching of history requires.

Amazing facts

Only one person is known with certainty to have been killed by the Fire.

Common misconceptions

The newly invented fire engines were crucial in putting out the fire.
Of course, every little helped, but the much-vaunted fire engines, quite unlike those we know today, were helpless in the face of such a fierce conflagration. The fire was defeated by a combination of dramatic measures (blowing up houses in the path of the fire and using additional troops) and luck, as the wind that fanned the flames died down.

● Write out some sentences outlining the main events of the fire and cut them out. The children could work in groups to sequence the sentences correctly. This could be made less difficult by using illustrations instead of, or to complement, the text.

● Groups of children could work to construct a class frieze of the Great Fire, based on contemporary engravings (widely reprinted in books on the period). This could be done effectively using silhouettes of buildings, red and orange paper for flames and cotton wool painted black and grey for smoke.

● Design a newspaper front page about the fire.

● Invite representatives from your local fire station to pay the school a visit and talk about their job.

● Work as a class to make a list of fire safety rules that would have helped to prevent the Great Fire of London. Tour the school examining your own fire precautions.

● Build models of the kind of wood-framed houses that were burned in the fire.

Samuel Pepys

Subject facts

Samuel Pepys only kept his famous diary for nine years, from 1660 to 1669. He stopped writing when his wife died and his eyesight began to fail.

The diary gives a vivid account of court intrigues and the problems Pepys experienced in naval administration – matters that he was deeply concerned about. It also gives an insight into the attitudes and culture of the time and, of course, a wonderful eyewitness account of the events of the Great Fire of London. The diary was written in a sort of mixture of code and shorthand to protect it from prying eyes. In it, Pepys was frank about his personal liaisons and feelings.

Pepys was an intelligent, educated man with considerable ability as an administrator and musician. His father was a London tailor but his father's cousin was the Earl of Sandwich, and it was with his help that Pepys got a job as a secretary to the Admiralty. His ability secured him promotion, although his supposed involvement in treasonable plots and corruption twice lost him his job. But Pepys was a survivor, and he rose to an important position in the Admiralty where he was hard-working and efficient. He was made President of the Royal Society in 1684.

In their own words

> *But Lord! What a sad sight it was by moonlight to see the whole City almost on fire – that you might see it plain at Woolwich as if you were by it.*

Samuel Pepys' Diary

Why you need to know these facts

Samuel Pepys is an important and influential historical figure whose diary remains an important source for the period in which he lived.

Teaching ideas

● Imitate Samuel Pepys. Write a diary of the events of the fire, pretending that you are a character living in London at the time – a maid, a firefighter, the Lord Mayor or a country visitor.
● The children could act out some of the events of the fire. Each group could be given the task of making a play of an aspect of the fire – the beginning, firefighters, refugees, Samuel Pepys and the Mayor, and the end. These could be performed as a class assembly.
● Samuel Pepys dug a deep hole to bury some of his valued possessions, including wine and Parmesan cheese. Ask the children to write about the precious things that they would hide if disaster threatened, and to explain their choices.

Resources

There is a lot of reference material about the fire available, but you do need to look beyond history books alone.

The Museum of London not only has splendid exhibits on the fire but also provides a wonderful online resource, where you can download a PDF of *What Happened in the Great Fire of London?*: **www.museumoflondon.org.uk**.

Follow the links to "Famous People" and "Samuel Pepys" in the Primary History pages on the BBC Schools Education website for lots of interesting background and pictures: **www.bbc.co.uk/schools/primaryhistory**.

There are lots of ready-made teaching resources on the TES website: **www.tes.co.uk**. As is usual with these sorts of resources, you will need to sift and sort to find what is suitable for you.

Books

For this project, even adult books about London can provide useful contextual information: *Kids' London* by Simon Adams (Dorling Kindersley, 2000) is a child-friendly, richly illustrated book worth finding, and even the brief tourist guide by the same publisher, *Top 10: London* (Dorling Kindersley, 2012), will help you find your way around.

You could put up a display of maps – one to show where London is, and another to show where the fire started and the extent of the damage. Bear in mind that a child's understanding of maps is very limited at this age.

Books about firemen abound for infants, and some contain information about fighting fires in the past. If you want to broaden the scope of the topic, or give it a more cross-curricular feel, then these books will be invaluable.

As for the event itself, fortunately this is one of those topics popular with publishers of books for children of this age group. There are also many aimed at older children that need not be dismissed just because the text is too demanding for the very young. You will need lots of pictures of London, of wood-framed houses and of 17th century streets. These books can provide just what you need. Here is a selection of some that are aimed at the young child, with simple bold text and clear illustrations:

- *The Great Fire of London* by Gillian Clements (Franklin Watts, 2002).
- *The Story of the Great Fire of London* by Jill Atkins (Wayland, 2008).
- *How Do We Know About the Great Fire of London?* by Deborah Fox (Raintree, 2004).
- *The Great Fire of London* by Sally Hewitt (Franklin Watts, 2004).

Visits

If your school is within the London area, then a visit to the Museum of London (**www.museumoflondon.org.uk**, 020 7001 9844), or a trip up the fire Monument is worth considering (but remember it has 311 steps!). If you are inexperienced at planning trips with young children, then do heed advice. In general, the further the trip, the less advisable it is to make it.

Want to know more?

If you want more background information yourself, or eyewitness accounts to quote to children, then you might consult the following. Most contain contemporary and other useful illustrations:

- I doubt whether you would want to look at the complete diaries of Pepys but *The Illustrated Pepys* by Robert Latham (Bell & Hyman, 1978) is still widely available, as is *The Diaries of Samuel Pepys: A Selection* (Penguin Classics, 2003).
- For a very comprehensive account, see: *The Great Fire of London* by Gustav Milne (Historical Publications, 1986).
- *Plague and Fire* by Leonard Cowie (Hodder Wayland, 1986) is a more accessible, blow-by-blow account.
- A recent detailed analysis is: *The Great Fire of London* by Stephen Porter (The History Press, 2009).

The following publishers' websites may also be helpful:

- **www.thehistorypress.co.uk** have specialised in publishing history books for a quarter of a century.
- **www.historicalpublications.co.uk** specialise in books on the history of London.

Chapter 3

Ancient Egypt

The key to understanding Egyptian history is the River Nile. Its fertile flood plain has supported the lives of settlers for over 5000 years of recorded history. The Nile delta (Lower Egypt) in the north is where the early Egyptian civilisation advanced most rapidly. The narrower Nile valley that stretches southwards was called Upper Egypt. The world's longest river, the Nile runs for 6738km (4187 miles). It gave birth to the civilisation of Ancient Egypt, a civilisation that lasted to the time of Roman rule in 30BC, a period of some 3000 years.

Introducing Ancient Egypt

Subject facts

Who were the Ancient Egyptians?
The people whom we usually refer to as Ancient Egyptians date from the time when the Lower and Upper parts of Egypt were united by Menes, the king of Upper Egypt, in around 3100BC. At the junction of the two united lands Menes established his capital city, later called Memphis (see Figure 1).

The first settlements around the River Nile, about a quarter of a million years ago, were probably just small hunting camps. But by 3500BC, the people of Lower and Upper Egypt were developing separately, and it seems that in Lower Egypt the people had discovered how to build structures that we would recognise as houses.

Timeline	
c.3100BC	Lower and Upper Egypt are united under one ruler (Menes).
2650–2400	The building of the pyramids.
2649–2150	The period of the Old Kingdom.
2134–1783	The Middle Kingdom.
1550–1070	The New Kingdom (Tuthmosis, Hatshepsut, Akhenaten, Tutankhamun, Rameses I–III).
1285	The battle of Kadesh (Rameses II claims victory over the Hittites).
724	Nubians occupy part of Egypt.
525	The Persians invade (Darius, Xerxes, Artaxerxes).
332	Alexander the Great conquers Egypt and drives out the Persians (Ptolemy I).
31	Battle of Actium against the Romans.
30	The Romans invade (Egypt is added to their Empire). Death of Cleopatra.

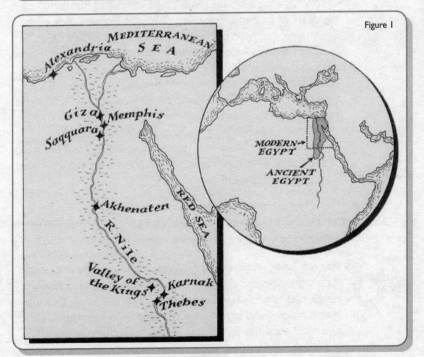

Figure 1

How do we know about the Ancient Egyptians?

At about the same time that Menes was uniting Egypt, the picture writing known as hieroglyphic text was invented. Historians therefore have evidence of these people, written on **papyrus** and stone. They also have the written evidence, eyewitness accounts and judgments of literate people who came into close contact with the Ancient Egyptians in later times, particularly the Greeks and Romans. Egypt is also mentioned in the Old Testament of the Bible (see the book of Genesis and the story of Joseph).

Huge structures (the temple at Abu Simbel and the pyramids at Giza for example), the contents of tombs, and the preserved bodies of the Ancient Egyptians themselves all provide a great deal of interesting detail about Ancient Egypt. We have furniture, games, paintings, jewellery, pottery, books and even textiles to study.

What happened to the Ancient Egyptians?

The Ancient Egyptian civilisation lasted for over 3000 years, and even survived the interruption of foreign rule by a number of conquerors: Ethiopians (**Nubians**), Greeks and Romans. But on the death of Queen Cleopatra in 30BC, the Romans took over. There were no more **pharaohs** and native rule ended. Egypt became part of a wider Mediterranean culture centred on Rome, but some cultural practices lingered on, and we know that the practice of mummification was not finally abandoned until some time in the 4th century AD. A 7th century invasion by Arabs made Egypt the predominantly Muslim country it is today.

Of their spoken language, which must have existed for thousands of years, very little remains. It is thought that the liturgy of the Coptic Christians has its root in ancient Egyptian, but we have no other legacy of their speech.

Why you need to know these facts

Ancient Egypt was one of the world's earliest civilisations, and as such it provides important clues about how the civilised world developed. Basic skills were developed in Ancient Egypt such as house building and farming. Ancient Egypt was the world's richest and most sophisticated ancient civilisation. It built the world's largest ancient buildings, the pyramids, and developed one of the world's earliest writing systems.

Primary children are generally fascinated by the Ancient Egyptians, making it an extremely popular topic with teachers. It is also a particularly useful topic as it introduces children, often for the first time, to the history of people living in a place beyond the British Isles.

Vocabulary

Nubians – came from southern Egypt and northern Sudan, an area that became Egyptianised, although Nubians did dominate Egypt in the 8th century BC.

Papyrus – a fleshy plant that used to grow in dense thickets in the Nile marshes. Thin strips were cut from the stem of the reed and laid side by side on flat stones. A second layer was laid at right angles on top. After being beaten with wooden mallets, a surface for writing on was produced.

Pharaoh – rulers or kings of Egypt. Pharaohs were so called because they lived in a palace called a great house or *per-ao*.

Egyptian society

Subject facts

Farming

The rhythm of Egyptian life was dictated by the Nile and its annual inundation. Between July and October, rains in central Sudan and Ethiopia raised the level of the river and caused it to flood, fertilising the land with a layer of silt. After the flood, the land was ploughed and crops sown. Tomb models have revealed that seeds were scattered by hand and farmers used oxen to draw their ploughs. Emmer wheat and barley (never corn) were sown – there were usually two successive crops harvested in April or May. Men gathered in the harvest while the women were responsible for winnowing the grain. They did this by tossing it in the air so the light stalks blew away and the heavy seeds fell to the ground. In Roman times the Egyptians were forced to grow more wheat and produce three harvests each year in order to feed Rome. Flax was the other main crop (this was used for linen, matting and rope), although vegetables, fruits and vines were cultivated in smaller plots.

From the river itself and the marshy delta areas, the Egyptians harvested fish and fowl, as well as papyrus and reeds for making papyrus scrolls, baskets and other domestic materials.

Artisans

From accounts and records we know that the Egyptians were skilled artists and workmen. They worked in stone, metal and wood, and produced fine objects in pottery, glass, precious metal and stone. All craftsmen served an apprenticeship, and virtually all worked directly or indirectly for the royal, government or temple workshops.

Writing

The Ancient Egyptians developed a system of writing called hieroglyphics that used pictures and signs which represented sounds, not words. Egyptian kings had their own hieroglyphs representing their names, known as **cartouches** (see Figure 2). How a word was pronounced would decide which hieroglyph would be used. Although the language has been deciphered we still have no clues as to how it was pronounced. The Ancient Egyptian alphabet comprised 24 basic signs that could be written from left to right, right to left, or top to bottom.

Figure 2

Houses

As always there was a difference between rich and poor homes. Houses of the poor were made with sun-baked mud bricks; houses of the wealthy were made of stone. The Egyptians mastered the art of working in stone at an early date: all the more permanent buildings were built of stone.

In general, houses were built on a square plan around a living room and had a flat roof. Their exteriors were whitewashed and the walls and floors inside could be painted, plastered or tiled. Larger, wealthier houses had bathrooms that consisted of a stone slab to stand on while washing, and there would have been an earth-closet toilet. For these ablutions poorer people used pots and bowls, which would be emptied some distance from the house. In larger urban areas, town houses could be two or three storeys and had high windows without glass.

It seems that many homes had some fitted furniture. Low platforms on which to sit or make up a bed were common. Wooden chests were used for storage and, besides the usual chairs and tables, extra comfort was provided by wall hangings, mats and cushions. All homes had places for statues of household gods.

The main meal of the day was taken in the evening, and was a family affair. Cooking was done over an open fire or in a pottery oven fuelled by straw, wood, leaves and animal dung. Bread, vegetables and fruits formed the basis of the Egyptian diet, and food was flavoured with garlic, herbs and spices, and sweetened using honey and dates. Wealthy Egyptians ate meat and fish mainly on special occasions. Beer made from barley was the most common drink (written records mention 17 varieties), although wine, milk and water were also drunk.

Leisure

Of course the Egyptians found some time to enjoy themselves, although most activities ended at dark when everyone went to bed. We know that children had simple toys and games such as spinning tops, balls, dolls and wooden animals, and adults took part in sports, dancing and making music. There were also several types of board game that they could play. The wealthy upper classes had more time for leisure and would entertain each other at banquets or go on hunting or fishing expeditions into the marshes or desert.

Warfare

The overwhelming impression one gets of life in Ancient Egypt is that of a peaceful agricultural existence, yet warfare interrupted the peace of the Nile Valley when powerful invaders sought to take the wealth of the Egyptians for themselves. But during the period of the New Kingdom, especially under Rameses III (1182–1151BC), the Egyptians were a powerful nation and made military forays into Palestine and beyond.

At the heart of the army were the infantry, who were armed with spears, shields and battleaxes. Rameses also used archers, mounted in horse-drawn chariots, to rain arrows down upon the enemy. The chariots were big enough to carry three men, and were drawn by two horses. The arrows had an estimated range of 200 metres (650 feet). The army was well organised, with different ranks of officers in charge of specific groups of men. Campaigns were fought in Nubia, Palestine and as far away as Syria.

Probably the most famous battle in Egyptian history is the battle of **Kadesh**, largely because it is so well recorded in sculptured reliefs. It was fought by Rameses II against the ancient enemies, the **Hittites**. In 1285BC Rameses stood with his army before the fortress of Kadesh in northern Syria. The Hittites, hidden behind the fortress, ambushed Rameses, who stood his ground with some 2500 chariots. At the last, victory (or at least a draw) at the battle of Kadesh was snatched from defeat by the arrival of reinforcements who attacked the Hittites from the rear.

The Egyptians had various enemies at different times. They were conquered by the Greeks under Alexander the Great (see Chapter 4, pages 54 and 72–3), by the Romans (see Chapter 5, pages 77–8) and by the Persians (see page 34). They fought against the Hittites, the Nubians and the Sea Peoples of the Mediterranean.

Why you need to know these facts

Children need to understand how events shaped the lives of people in the past, and that such changes took place within the period when the Ancient Egyptian civilisation flourished.

Vocabulary

Cartouche – groups of Egyptian hieroglyphs contained within an oval shape, indicating a royal or divine name.

Hittites – powerful enemies of the Egyptians around 1650BC, their empire centered on modern Turkey and Syria.

Irrigation – the provision of water by the use of artificial canals to land lacking in moisture, in order to grow crops.

Kadesh – site in northern Syria of the great battle between Rameses II and the Hittites. Rameses claimed the victory although it was indecisive. The Arabic is *Qadesh* but Kadesh is acceptable and easier to pronounce.

Nilometer – a graduated stone used by the Ancient Egyptians to measure flood levels.

Rosetta Stone – this provided the key which enabled scholars to read Ancient Egyptian hieroglyphs. It was discovered at Rashid (Rosetta) in the Nile delta in AD1799. The inscription on the stone was in hieroglyphs, demotic script and Greek. It still took over 20 years to decipher it – an achievement credited to Jean Champollion in 1822.

Amazing facts

● We have no evidence of any Ancient Egyptian woman who learned to read or write.

● Papyrus does not grow anywhere naturally in Egypt today. The tourist trade in papyrus is largely met by using 'paper' made with banana skins.

● Animals were often part of Egyptian households, and cats in particular were highly revered. When a pet cat died the whole family would shave off their eyebrows as a sign that they were in mourning.

● Wall and tomb paintings have revealed what the Ancient Egyptians wore. The most common material was white linen made from flax, which the men wore as loincloths and the women as long dresses. Leather or reed sandals were worn.

Children wore few clothes, and in many paintings are shown naked with their heads shaved, leaving one or two long locks of hair called 'locks of youth'.

Common misconceptions

There were few trees in Egypt, so all timber had to come from the Lebanon.

In fact there were (and are) many trees in Egypt. Pollen analysis by archaeologists has shown that all types of trees existed in Egypt (hardwood, softwood, deciduous and coniferous) and that it always had lots of native wood.

The Egyptians spoke hieroglyphics.

Hieroglyphs were written symbols, but the spoken language was Ancient Egyptian. Nobody knows what it sounded like, although Coptic, surviving only in the liturgical language of the Coptic Church, has its roots in Ancient Egyptian.

Teaching ideas

- Get the children to design a picture strip cartoon showing a day in the life of an Egyptian farmer.
- Children could design a cartouche of their name.
- Get the children to write an account of a hunting trip – undertaking some research first. It could be into the marshes, or perhaps the desert.
- Read a story from the Old Testament about the Egyptians, such as 'Joseph and his coat of many colours'.
- Conduct a class discussion about life in Ancient Egypt. One group should argue in favour of life in those times, while another points out the disadvantages.
- The children could copy the Egyptian style of painting. They could depict themselves and their family and pets or an important event from their lives.

Beliefs, burial and the afterlife

Subject facts

Gods

The pattern of Egyptian belief was very different from the Romans or Greeks and is quite complicated. You can divide Egyptian gods into four groups:

● First there were the gods of the cosmos – the stars and heaven – that were included in Ancient Egyptian mythology but were not worshipped.

● Then there were 'domestic' deities, which equated closely to modern superstitions – amulets that protected or brought good luck. Also not part of any system of worship.

● Next there were the gods of the dead (Figure 3). These judged people's actions in life and ruled the *Duat*, or underworld. These were only worshipped towards the end of the Ancient Egyptian period, when Egypt was strongly under the influence of Greece and Rome.

Figure 3

ANUBIS   HORUS   OSIRIS   ISIS   THOTH   BASTET

● Finally there were the local, and most important, gods. These were worshipped because they were believed to bring benefit to their local place. The local god (simply referred to as 'God' in most cases) was the only one of any relevance in the lives of the people, so the Egyptians were, in a sense, monotheistic. Souls of the ancient dead of a place formed these gods because they were thought to be benevolent towards their own locality.

Worship, in the form of offerings three times a day, was really a kind of deal, an act of barter. It was not about prayer or praise; if a god failed to deliver he might be cursed, a broken promise written on a pot and then smashed against a wall.

The Egyptians never worshipped animals or thought of their gods as having animal heads. When animal-headed gods were portrayed on temple walls, this was to explain to illiterate people the characteristic of the god (a kind of visual metaphor), and the pictures were used rather as wall paintings on the walls of medieval churches were used.

If you wanted to make a special request to a god, it was thought that they would take more notice of one of their creatures than of the plea of a mere mortal. So creatures were bred in the temple for sale, slaughter and mummification. Placed in a pot, their souls were thought to fly straight to the god with the person's request.

The journey to heaven

If you wanted to live forever in the company of Osiris, King of the Dead, in a pleasant land (like Egypt) with rich harvests of grain (but no work to do), you had to make a journey through the underworld. At the end of the journey, and before you could qualify for eternal life, your heart was weighed by the god Anubis against the feather of truth. This was to see how well you had behaved on Earth. If it weighed too much, there was a monster called Ammit ('devourer of the dead') ready to eat it. The journey was a kind of obstacle course, with a crocodile to avoid as well as an incredible serpent, a fierce fire, and a monkey with a trap. To make this journey easier, a collection of around 200 magic spells was written, called the '**Book of the Dead**'. Copies of these sheets of papyrus were placed in tombs or between the layers of bandages of a mummy, near the legs.

The Egyptian heaven was perceived as part of two earths that ran in parallel. The Ancient Egyptians lived in the top one and the afterlife was below. The Sun travelled across their sky, then set to travel across the sky of the afterlife, before returning at dawn.

Mummies

The Egyptians loved living and were not obsessed with death. They saw death as an extension of life, which was good. They expected all the good things to continue after they died.

However, for the journey to the afterlife to be negotiated successfully it was best, so they thought, that the body was preserved; if the body was destroyed the spirit might be lost. So those people of wealth or status, such as pharaohs and the nobility, had their bodies mummified by priests.

The word 'mummy' comes from an Arabic word for bitumen (mummified bodies are black in appearance) and has nothing to do with parenthood. We know how the process worked from X-ray and other examinations of the bodies, but chiefly from the writings of the Greek, Herodotus, who wrote a description of the process, which he observed on his travels around Egypt in 450BC.

It took the priests 70 days to mummify a body. The liver, lungs, stomach and intestines were removed and placed in special 'canopic' jars. Only the heart was left in place, as this was felt to be essential for the journey to the afterlife. It was a lengthy, delicate, messy and smelly process. The brain was removed through the nostrils by a hook. All the moisture had to be removed to ensure preservation, and this was done by washing the body in palm wine and then covering it in **natron**, a naturally occurring salt. After 40 days, the embalmers would rub the skin with oils and pack the body with spices, linen, sawdust and sand to reshape it. Finally, they would wrap it in layers of bandages soaked in resin. Magic spells and amulets were often folded into the layers to bring good luck in the afterlife. Then the mummy was sealed in its case.

The process was finished off before entombment with ceremonies and prayers. A collection of useful artefacts for the afterlife, such as prayers, food, **shabti** and furniture, was placed with the mummy. *Shabti* were pottery figures representing the servants who would carry out the agricultural duties that would be demanded of the deceased, so they were very important objects in the tomb. The tombs of the great pharaohs have yielded incredible treasures of great value, but the wealth buried with the pharaohs was a considerable temptation to thieves and most tombs that we know of were robbed at some time. Only a fraction of what was buried has survived to modern times.

Pyramids

For about 100 years pharaohs were buried in pyramids, but because of their size they could not be hidden, so the tombs were easily robbed. We know of 88 pyramids, and all but two are bare inside. Clever though they were in their construction, sometimes with false doors, tunnels and dead ends, thieves always managed to get in eventually, because the prize was so great and the temptation irresistible.

Then, in about 1500BC, the idea developed of hiding the tomb as well as the treasure. For the next 500 years pharaohs cut into the stone floor and wall of a secret valley to the west of **Luxor** to create their burial places. This valley, known as the 'Valley of the Kings', is surrounded by high cliffs. It is hidden away from the Nile on its western side.

These hidden tombs have wonderfully decorated walls, replete with paintings of kings. Although some were robbed, others, such as the tomb of Tutankhamun (see page 48), have been found virtually intact. Perhaps some have yet to be found and hold their secrets still.

Building the pyramids

Large numbers of people were needed to build the pyramids. At Giza, archaeologists have found homes for 8000 people, which are thought to be those of the workers who built the pyramids. The stone was cut in quarries and moved by boat crews of 60 divided into four groups of 15 men. Each group had a daily quota of stone to move – a quota that was never met!

Giza is particularly notable for its pyramids because there, on the edge of the desert, 9 kilometres (6 miles) from Cairo, stands the largest of all – the Great Pyramid. It is the last surviving of the seven wonders of the ancient world. It was built around 2550BC from limestone and faced with finer limestone from across the Nile at Tura. The workers used ropes attached to smooth wooden rollers coated in fine mud to help haul the massive blocks of stone across the desert. Each block of stone, put in place by hand, weighed 25,000 kilograms – about the weight of an adult male hippopotamus. There were 2,300,000 such blocks. The Great Pyramid stood 146.6 metres (481 feet) high originally, and the error of alignment of the base is only half a degree at the maximum. It was a tomb for King Cheops (the Egyptians call him Khufu).

Why you need to know these facts

Mummies, pyramids and the tombs of pharaohs provide us with some of our most significant evidence about the Ancient Egyptians. The pyramids are also worthy of study in their own right, as one of the ancient wonders of the world.

Vocabulary

Book of the Dead – in Ancient Egypt the journey of the spirit in the afterlife was recorded on papyrus known as the 'Book of the Dead'. The journey showed the blissful world of the Egyptian heaven, a land like the Nile, rich in wildlife and food. The Egyptians called it 'The Book of the Coming into Day'.

Luxor – the home town of the kings of the Ancient Egyptian New Kingdom from around 1550BC onwards. They built their palaces here and chose to be buried in the rock-cut tombs of the Valley of the Kings (sometimes referred to as Thebes).

Natron – a whitish, yellow mineral that occurs in salt lakes. Used by the Ancient Egyptians to dry out fluids in corpses undergoing mummification.

Shabti – also *ushabti*; in Ancient Egypt, models of workers that were buried with mummies and who would spring to life on the command of Osiris to do the work required of the mummified person on their journey through the afterlife.

Amazing facts

● Some people believe in the curse of the pyramids. After Howard Carter excavated the tomb of Tutankhamun in 1922, this belief became very popular. Although Lord Cannar died of an infected mosquito bite shortly after the excavation, both Howard Carter and the young boy who was the first to enter the burial chamber lived well into old age.

● Experiments by Japanese egyptologists have shown that, by using a ramp of 12 degrees – as given on mathematical papyri –

a block of stone weighing 25,000kg could be dragged on a sledge by eight men with little difficulty; but we do not know precisely how the pyramids and obelisks were built.

Common misconceptions

That there were slaves in ancient Egypt.
If we define a slave as a person with no identity or rights before the law, then these did not exist. Every person – male, female, foreigner or native – had equal rights under the law. Even prisoners in battle, although handed out as rewards to brave soldiers, still had rights. However, everyone was a servant (all worked directly or indirectly for the state). Pharaoh himself was referred to as 'god's servant'. The emotive term 'slave' – a person with no rights – cannot be applied until Roman times, when the Romans enslaved the Egyptians.

Teaching ideas

- Using clay for the base, get the children to make a papier mâché replica of the mask of Tutankhamun.
- Tell the children, 'You are pharaoh – prepare to meet thy tomb'. Get the children to make an inventory of all the objects they would like to be buried with when they die.
- Some say that disturbing the graves of people buried long ago is wrong. Have a class debate about this.
- The pyramids were ancient monuments even in the time of the later Egyptians. Get the children to describe a day out to the pyramids as if they were a child being taken by their father to visit them 2500 years ago.
- As a class, build a scale model of the Great Pyramid at Giza. Check all the measurements first. Can the children work out the mathematical net of a pyramid?
- Make a wall display about the seven wonders of the ancient world.
- Investigate Anubis, Horus, Re, Thoth and Sakhmet. How many other Egyptian gods can the children find out about?

Important people and places

Subject facts

The land

The most powerful people in Ancient Egypt were the pharaohs, who were kings of Egypt and who ruled as absolute monarchs. The source of their power was land – all land belonged to the pharaohs. If they gave land to anyone it was actually only the produce of the land that was given and not the land itself, and even this produce could be taxed. At the time, 98 per cent of people worked on the land, so ownership of land equalled power.

The rich Nile valley was the most important place to the Egyptians – they called it the 'Black Land', because each year when the Nile was in flood, thick, dark mud was washed over the banks. This soil alongside the river was very fertile and was used to grow crops. To the east and west lay the deserts, and these were referred to as the 'Red Land'. Here there was nothing but vast stony wastes where rain was scarce and nothing grew.

The great pharaohs

Hatshepsut, 1498–1483BC
(all early dates are approximate)
Hatshepsut married her half-brother Tuthmosis II, and when he died she should not have become pharaoh, as succession was through the male line. But nevertheless she took over government for her five-year-old stepson Tuthmosis III, for whom she was supposed to be acting as regent. Hers was a peaceful and culturally rich reign – she seems to have been a woman of considerable strength of character (she is often portrayed as male), and held on to government for about 20 years, until her death.

Akhenaten, 1350–1334BC
He introduced many changes to the lives of his people, not least of which was to abandon the old religion with its many gods. Akhenaten was a monotheist – that is, he believed that there was

only one god: Aten, the Sun god. The old temples in the area of Tel el Amarna were closed down and Akhenaten built a new capital, 300 kilometres (186 miles) down the Nile from the old city of Thebes (see Figure 1 on page 33). The new capital was also called Akhenaten and was dedicated to the Sun god. But there is no evidence that Akhenaten imposed monotheism on his people, nor that he worshipped the Sun as God – rather he used the Sun as a metaphor for God. Some people moved north to set up new homes there, but the new capital only lasted for about 15 years, and after Akhenaten's death they moved back to their old homes and returned to the old religion again.

Nefertiti, 14th century BC (ruled with Akhenaten, see the previous page and above)

Half-sister of Tutankhamun, she was married to Akhenaten, and appears to have been a powerful influence, especially in encouraging monotheism. She effectively ruled with Akhenaten. Their successors took exception to their disparaging of the old gods and tried to obliterate their memory by removing their names from inscriptions and pulling down their temples.

Tutankhamun, 1334–1325BC

A boy ruler – he was only nine when he came to the throne – who achieved immortality largely because of the discovery of his tomb and extensive grave goods. The tomb was found in 1922 and entered in February 1923 by Howard Carter. Tutankhamun's tomb had been robbed (the footprints of the robbers were found), but the robbers were probably caught in the act and most of the tomb seemed intact. His famous gold-masked coffin was encased in two other coffins.

Rameses II (The Great), 1279–1212BC

His victory over arch-enemies the Hittites in the battle of Kadesh (in Syria) is recorded on many reliefs, although it was not as decisive as the celebratory sculptures might suggest. Rameses built the huge temple at Abu Simbel and more statues than any other pharaoh. He ruled for 67 years.

Ptolemy Soter, 323–285BC

Alexander the Great's general became ruler of Egypt when
Alexander died in 323BC. Ptolemy ruled Egypt from Alexandria.
He founded a Greek-speaking dynasty that ruled for 300 years in
the same way as traditional Egyptian rulers. Ptolemy spent much
of his reign defending the frontiers of his land, and earned himself
the title *Soter*, which means saviour. He abdicated in 285BC in
favour of his son. He died in 283BC.

Cleopatra, 69–30BC

Cleopatra was the last Greek pharaoh (the last of the Ptolemy
dynasty). She lost her throne in a palace coup, but was restored
to power by Julius Caesar. She formed a political and personal
alliance with Marc Antony by whom she bore three children.
Marc Antony was apparently completely besotted with Cleopatra
and left his wife and children for her, but ambition brought them
into conflict with Rome and Marc Antony's infatuation lost him
public respect and support. They were defeated by the Romans
under Augustus at the battle of Actium in 31BC. After her lover
Antony had died in her arms, she killed herself by taking poison,
possibly by causing a snake to bite her breast.

Why you need to know these facts

History is primarily about people, and the most significant
people in Ancient Egypt, about whom substantial evidence
exists, are the pharaohs. To understand the Ancient Egyptians,
we must learn about pharaohs.

Amazing facts

There must have been a great deal of consent in the exercise
of power by the pharaohs because there are few records of
assassinations, and when an assassination did happen it was
usually to dispose of a usurper.

Ancient Egypt

Common misconceptions

Cleopatra was beautiful.
This idea dates from Tudor times. Her contemporaries thought she was plump and plain but that she had great charm, wit and intelligence.

The Ancient Egyptians looked like white Europeans.
This was clearly not so. The Nubians from the south formed part of Egypt at one time, and they were African. Painted limestone statues of government officials show men having darker skin than women. This was normal practice: women were expected to have less exposure to the Sun and thus were always depicted with paler skins in murals.

Teaching ideas

- On an outline map of the eastern Mediterranean, mark all the places of significance in the history of Ancient Egypt.
- Design a travel poster advertising the tourist sites worth visiting in modern Egypt.
- Choose a famous Egyptian pharaoh and write an obituary for him or her listing all their achievements.
- Study the geography of the River Nile, then write an encyclopaedia entry giving as much data as possible. Look at climate, land use and physical geography.
- Pretend that the Egyptian 'style' has become fashionable. Design a range of goods (clothes, furniture, objects) for sale in a well-known shop.
- Imagine you are in jail: you were a tomb robber caught in the act. Describe the events of the ill-fated robbery.

Resources

First-hand experience of the evidence is not so easy when dealing with a country in Africa, unless your children have visited the key sites in Egypt. However, there are a great number of artefacts in British museums, especially in the British Museum itself, which of course has many, including the **Rosetta Stone** and a number of mummies. In the 19th and 20th centuries, many European archaeologists removed material from ancient sites and brought it back to European museums, which is why, if you cannot go to Egypt, you will find that much of it has come to you. Your local museum may well surprise you.

For visits to the British Museum in Great Russell Street, London contact the museum information desk by calling 020 7323 8299 or emailing **learning@britishmuseum.org**. The British Museum produces downloadable material specifically aimed at primary children. There is also a free image service. Consult **www.britishmuseum.org/learning.aspx**. Postcards, charts and activity books are also available from the Museum.

The Manchester Museum has one of the largest collections of Egyptian artefacts in the country and a new gallery opened in October 2012. Lots of help and information is available here: **www.museum.manchester.ac.uk/learning/informationforteachers**

A major and little-visited collection can be seen in the Petrie Museum of Egyptian Archaeology, University College, Gower Street, London WC1E 6BT (telephone: 020 7679 2000). The museum welcomes school visits (though note opening times are limited). There is a downloadable teacher's pack called 'Egypt in Africa' available here: **www.ucl.ac.uk/museums/petrie**

The Smithsonian Institute in Washington has a good website with excellent material and information, including extensive booklists of children's and other books: **www.si.edu**

Remember, you do not need to go to Washington: local is best. The Dorset County Museum in Dorchester will serve as an example: **www.dorsetcountymuseum.org**

For pictures and other teaching resources you should, of course, check out sites that you will be familiar with (TES, DfES, Child Education, etc.).

Downloadable pictures from the Dorling Kindersley Clip Art selection can be accessed at: **www.clipart.dk.co.uk/subjects**

Ancient Egypt

Books

Egypt is a popular topic; consequently there are many reference books for children, although there are variations in the quality of scholarship so don't be too surprised if children find factual differences between books. Once again, the British Museum is an excellent source. Books do come and go, but out-of-print volumes live on for some time in library collections, so do check. The following are readily available:

- *The Ancient Egyptians Activity Book* by Lise Manniche (British Museum Press, 1999).
- *Pyramid Activity Book* by Delia Pemberton (British Museum Press, 2003).
- *Eyewitness: Ancient Egypt* by George Hart (Dorling Kindersley, 2007) is obtainable with wallchart and clipart CD. This well-tested DK formula works particularly well for this topic, and is packed with information that can be accessed on a number of levels.
- *Ancient Egypt* by Miranda Smith (Kingfisher, 2010) is vivid and attractive.
- *An Egyptian Pyramid* by J. Morley, M. Bergin and J. James (Book House, 2011).
- *Ancient Egypt* by Jane Shuter (Heinemann Library, 2005), is well-produced and detailed.
- *The Egyptians* by Sally Hewitt (Hodder, 2010) is for younger readers.
- *Egyptian Town* by S. Steedman and D. Antram (Franklin Watts, 1998) is graphically different, with detailed bird's eye views. Worth it if you can find a copy.

Want to know more?

Even a short search will reveal that many books have been written on this subject, often with excellent illustrations. Here are three to get you started:

- *The British Museum Concise Introduction: Ancient Egypt* by T. G. H. James (British Museum Press, 2005) is a colourful book written by the expert at the British Museum.
- *The Rise and Fall of Ancient Egypt* by Toby Wilkinson (Bloomsbury, 2011) is a weighty academic paperback.
- *Egypt* by J. Tyldesley (Templar, 2007) is a colourful source book.

Chapter 4

The Ancient Greeks

Today the Olympic Games is probably the only festival that is truly worldwide, and yet it is just one small legacy of a people who gave us not only the essentials of democracy and modern civilisation, but also the very words to describe them. For us, the story of the Ancient Greeks begins around 800 years before the birth of Christ, when the names of winners at the Olympic Games were first written down. Before that moment, we have only the silent and limited evidence of archaeology to bear witness to the world of the Ancient Greeks.

Introducing the Ancient Greeks

Subject facts

Who were the Ancient Greeks?

The Greek civilization developed mainly in small **city states** (see pages 68–9), and predominantly in the states of Athens and Sparta. The Ancient Greek city states had frequent quarrels and violent disputes with each other, and were never united as a single nation. However, the people were bound by a common language, religion and culture. The Greeks called themselves *Hellenes* and their country *Hellas*. Their civilization reached its height in Athens in the 4th and 5th centuries BC. It was during this period that the Greeks produced their great literature and architecture, and developed world-changing ideas, such as democracy.

With numerous islands and mountainous terrain, Greece covers only 80,650km², yet the Greeks colonized land from southern Russia to Libya and from Spain to Turkey and Syria.

Under the leadership of Alexander the Great (see pages 72–3), Greek culture spread via conquest to what is now West Pakistan.

So Classical Greece is particularly hard to pin down to one place, and some historians have even suggested that it should be regarded as an idea rather than a physical entity – it tended to be wherever Greek was spoken.

With the conquests of Alexander the Great, the Greek world expanded and moved its centre eastwards in what is known as the 'Hellenistic period' (323–146BC).

Timeline (The dates for these ancient times are approximate)	
776BC (traditionally)	First written record of the Olympic Games.
700	First **triremes** built.
7th century BC	The use of metal coins spread from modern Turkey to being used all over the Greek world. Beginning of the city states and the expansion of the Greek world.
594	Reforms of Solon – beginning of democracy in Athens.
534	First drama festival held in Athens.
508	Clisthenes reorganised the government of Athens so that full power lay with the Citizen Assembly. He called the system one of equal rights (isonomia), but created what was essentially the first democracy. The word 'democracy' came in to general use in the 5th century BC.
492–449	Wars against the Persian Empire.
490	Battle of Marathon. The marathon race was introduced to the Olympic Games after a soldier had run over 42 kilometres (26 miles) from Marathon to Athens to inform the city of a victory over the Persians. He dropped dead on arrival.
480	Battle of Salamis: Greek victory over a Persian fleet which outnumbered them by three to one. Battle of Thermopylae: the Spartans under King Leonidas held the pass against the invading Persians, led by Xerxes. The Greeks were betrayed and outflanked; Leonidas sent away most of his army before they became trapped and stayed with 300 men to hold off the Persians. They were all killed. Xerxes nailed Leonidas' body to a cross.

Timeline (The dates for these ancient times are approximate)	
479	Battle of Plataea.
431–404	Peloponnesian War between Sparta and Athens and their allies.
359	Philip of Macedon (Alexander the Great's father) comes to power and begins his domination of the Greek world.
338	Philip defeats the Athenians and their allies and gains mastery over Greece.
331	Alexander defeats Darius III at the battle of Gaugamela. End of the Persian Empire.
327	Alexander enters India via the Khyber Pass.
323	Death of Alexander the Great in Babylon.
After 323BC	In the 300 years to the death of Cleopatra in 30BC, Greek civilisation spread across the known world, but political independence ended. Dominance of the world passed to the Romans.

Figure 4

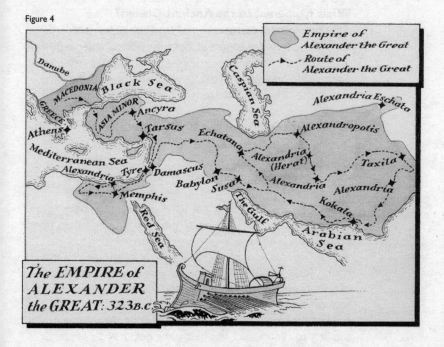

How do we know about the Ancient Greeks?

In the Classical period the Greeks had a fully developed alphabet, so their voices can speak to us across the ages through the written word. The records of Greek traders, writers, politicians and poets give us insights into their intellectual as well as their physical lives. We need to be wary though – all our information about Sparta comes largely from Athenian writers because the Spartans did not write histories or other books.

Archaeology, coupled with ever-improving scientific techniques, provides a mass of evidence, not only through the tools, weapons and artefacts unearthed, but also through the skilful interpretation and re-interpretation of the sites where they were found.

Myth, legend and both oral and written traditions are also valuable to the historian and yield further insights.

Not only have we the Greeks' fine architecture to remind us of their skill, but also jewellery, artefacts and many vases, which yield useful evidence about society and what the Ancient Greeks actually looked like.

What happened to the Ancient Greeks?

After the death of Alexander in 323BC, Greek ideas and civilisation continued to spread, but their political independence ended and the Romans became rulers of the world. However, many ideas and aspects of the Western way of life today have their roots in Ancient Greece.

What is the legacy of the Ancient Greeks?

The influence of Greek culture on Western society today is greater than that of any other nation in history. Many banks, town halls and prestigious buildings exhibit columns and pediments taken directly from Greek designs, and there is hardly an area of intellectual activity – literature, science, aesthetics, politics or philosophy – on which Greek ideas have not had a fundamental impact:

● The Greeks invented the literary forms of epic poetry and drama. Aeschylus, Sophocles and Euripides were great tragic playwrights of the 5th century BC, and Aristophanes was a memorable comic poet and dramatist.

● Herodotus is called 'the father of history' because he was the first to reconstruct the past using documentary records rather than relying on myths and legends. He wrote a history of the Persian Wars. Thucydides wrote a history of the Peloponnesian Wars in which he was an eyewitness, but he also discussed causes and sought to draw general conclusions about events.

● Philosophy originated in Ancient Greece and was raised to an art form in the dialogues of Plato, who was a pupil of Socrates. Socrates died without ever writing a word (his beliefs are known through the writings of his pupils Plato and Xenophon), but he turned philosophy into discussions about the nature of man, morals and the universe. Aristotle followed Plato and was a considerable influence on the thinkers of the Middle Ages. He also initiated biological studies based upon the collection of data. The philosophers (or stoics) of the Hellenistic period focused on virtue and living according to Divine Will, and clearly affected the way in which Christianity developed.

● On the island of Kos, the Hippocratic School of Physicians invented medicine as a scientific art. Archimedes calculated the value of *pi*; Aristarchus worked out that the Sun was larger than the Earth and that the planets revolved around the Sun; Eratosthenes calculated the circumference of the Earth to within a margin of 322 kilometres (200 miles). The Greeks used **machines**, such as the screw and the cogwheel, and even used steam power and air pressure.

● In art and architecture they made revolutionary strides and produced the West's first naturalist sculpture and painting. Their architecture, with its columns and classical orders, had an influence that endures still.

● The notion that every citizen was a potential politician, and that the business of government was therefore of interest to everyone, was a Greek one. The Greeks effectively invented not only democracy (usually dated from the reforms of Solon in Athens c573BC) but politics itself. Plato and Aristotle developed political theory and the concept of the ideal state.

● Perhaps more tangible legacies, from the children's point of view, are to be found in the words we use. Suffixes and prefixes such as -ology, -phobia, tech-, geo-, photo-; names like Alexander, Helen, Nike and Mars, and words such as 'stadium' and 'dinosaur' are all within the child's experience. The children will also have heard Greek myths and legends and, of course, be familiar with the Olympic Games.

The Ancient Greeks

> **Some modern words that have their root meaning in Ancient Greek:**
> **Aristocracy** – rule of the best born.
> **Democracy** – rule of the people.
> **Geometry** – to measure the land.
> **Machine** – a device.
> **Philosophy** – love of wisdom.
> **Physics** – nature.
> **Politics** – from 'citizen' (*polis* = city).

● The Greeks were responsible for our alphabet's evolution into a flexible and powerful tool, and for passing it on to the Romans.

Why you need to know these facts

Almost every part of western European culture owes some debt to the Greeks. From sport and medicine to politics and architecture, from drama and literature to philosophy and mathematics, the influence of the Ancient Greeks has been fundamental and can still be felt today. For this reason the story of Ancient Greece justifies its place in the school curriculum. The history of Greece forms part of our history. The links to a primary child's experience are easy to make. Through their holidays, the Olympic Games, architecture and mythological stories, for example, children can learn about the achievements, the way of life and the legacy of Ancient Greek civilisation.

Vocabulary

City state – a unit of government and settlement (*polis* in Greek). Athens, Sparta and Thebes are examples from Ancient Greece.
Triremes – Greek galley warships that dominated the Mediterranean well into Roman times; powered by oarsmen in units of three.

Ancient Greek society

Subject facts

Life was simple by modern standards: it was hard, short and often brutal. We would probably regard the Greek way of life as primitive, yet it still had intellectual power and vitality that astonishes us even today.

Architecture

When we think of Ancient Greece we often think first of great stone buildings, such as the **Parthenon**, with their grand columns. The Parthenon was built on the **Acropolis** in Athens as a shrine to the goddess Athena (see page 67), and no expense was spared in its construction. Within the Parthenon the Athenians erected a statue to Athena carved by Pheidias, an acclaimed sculptor. It towered 11 metres (36 feet) high and was richly decorated with gold and ivory. The Parthenon was finished in 432BC after 15 years of work. The columns supporting the roof were in the Doric style (tapering fluted columns and round, undecorated capitals) commonly used on mainland Greece. The Ionic style had slender columns and scroll capitals, and was used in the Greek cities in Turkey. Both styles were in use in the 5th century BC. The Corinthian style (highly decorated capitals, used greatly by the Romans) came in to use at the end of the century.

Houses

It is difficult to get a clear picture of Greek houses because they were largely made of sun-dried brick laid on stone foundations, and have not survived. They appear to have been quite simple structures, roofed with terracotta tiles, with separate areas for women and children. Town houses were probably more grand with a greater number of rooms.

Life expectancy

Everyone had to work to live and there were not too many surpluses to support the old, the sick or the weak – your family was your only lifeline. Life expectancy for men was around

35 years. Women, because of the risks of childbirth, could not expect to live so long. Death rates among babies were extremely high. Slaves, particularly those working in the Athenian silver mines, had a short life expectancy.

Slaves

Quality of life depended then, as now, on who you were. Slaves were at the bottom of the social ladder and were not only captives of war but could also be debtors sold into slavery in payment for money owed; this was sometimes used as a quick way of raising capital. Solon – credited with the founding of democracy – brought in, as part of his famous reforms (see the timeline on page 54), a law cancelling agricultural debts and emancipated all Athenians sold into slavery. Slaves had a pretty poor existence, although some lived as well as poorer citizens in the cities. At one point there were more than 20,000 slaves in Athens and its silver mines. Some slaves were Greek, but most came from barbarian tribes. The police of Athens were Scythian archers – state slaves bought in south Russia.

In their own words

Slaves and the lower classes are treated very freely here. No one beats a slave or expects him to stand aside in the street to let him pass. Athenians dress no better than slaves, so if there was a law saying that you could beat a slave one would often beat a citizen by mistake.

Pseudo-Xenophon I,
5th century BC

Women

Women were the largest underclass: they were ignored politically and many hardly ever left the home. Girls would be married off at 13 or 14 years of age as result of financial or political deals arranged by men, and the bride was excluded from the celebration. Wives could be beaten, even killed with impunity. Legally they had few rights but they did hold important domestic power in richer houses, supervising the household and its complement of slaves. Their social position varied, and Sappho (see page 74) and the women of Lesbos seem to have enjoyed greater freedom than other Greek women (Sappho's poetry is still admired today). Women and slaves were expected to wait on men when they held drinking parties called *symposia*. Female slaves then danced while the respectable women withdrew.

Food

Diet again depended upon wealth, but bread and porridge were staple foods. Fruit and vegetables were eaten in large quantities when in season (apples, pears, pomegranates and figs) but meat was largely reserved for special occasions. Fish was a popular food, especially in towns near the sea. Hunting and fishing were important pastimes, as Greek soil is mainly poor and a great deal of effort was required to provide a useful crop. Wine was everybody's drink and both rich and poor consumed large quantities, usually diluted with water.

Clothes

Vase pictures in particular give us a very good idea about what the normal citizen wore. Bearing in mind the hot climate of Greece, it comes as no surprise that both men and women wore wide-brimmed hats. Most clothing was loose and free and thin, woven from fine wool. The loose cloak worn by everybody was known as a *chiton*. It could be tucked up short by workmen or wrapped around the body and worn to ground length by women. Both men and women wore leather sandals.

Education

In about 800BC, the Greeks improved the Phoenician alphabet by including vowels as well as consonants. Written language was then made much easier and it was possible for anyone to learn how to read and write. Written laws, argument, poetry and stories could replace or complement those that had been passed on orally, and a man's store of knowledge ceased being limited to the capacity of his memory. The advances made in Greek learning and literature owe much to this one invention.

Education was given only to boys from about seven years of age and they were taught what we erroneously call the 'three Rs' – reading, writing and arithmetic. Like the Romans in a later period, the Greeks used a stylus (a sharp writing implement) pressed into a wax tablet to write down their work. Music, poetry and debating were also part of their education, and physical education was of major importance as a preparation for war. Rich families might have their girls privately educated but most learned only domestic tasks, such as how to spin and weave.

The Olympic Games

Sport started as part of religious celebrations. The Olympic Games were invented by the Greeks over 2500 years ago (tradition has it, in 776BC): sport and religion were mixed in a festival held every four years at Olympia to honour the god Zeus. In Roman times, the growth of Christianity gradually killed off the old pagan festivals and the ancient Olympics were finally ended by the Roman Emperor Theodosius in AD371. The modern Olympic Games started in 1896 and the first were held in Athens. There were also games festivals held in Corinth – the Isthmian – and in Delphi – the Nemean and the Pythian. Collectively these festivals are known as the Panhellenic Games. Throughout the 5th century BC the Olympics were the biggest competition of all and lasted for five days. Even wars sometimes stopped to allow the games to take place.

There were many similarities with today's Games. The athletes trained hard, had special diets and coaches and sometimes cheated. Cheats in the ancient Games were considered to have insulted the gods. They were punished by whipping-men if caught, and the city they represented was fined. You had to be Greek and a free man in order to compete in the games, which were an all-male affair – women could not even watch. Nudity was the norm (possibly as a means of making sure that no female could compete in disguise), physical prowess was much admired and the perfect body idolised in statues and paintings. Some historians believe that Spartan women competed regularly in their own athletic competitions. They certainly received physical training in order to build up their strength to produce fine babies.

Some of the events would still be recognised today, such as throwing the discus. Others, like the long jump, have changed a little – Greek long jumpers carried weights in their hands to help propel them a long distance. There were five key competitions in the Olympics: discus, javelin, wrestling, running and long jump; these made up the pentathlon. More and more events were added to the games – boxing and mud-wrestling were very popular and, after the battle of Marathon, the marathon was included as an event. Winners were awarded a palm branch and large jars of oil. Then, on the final day of the games, they were crowned with olive wreaths. Athletes winning three or more events were allowed to have a statue put up in their honour, with an inscription that recorded their success.

In their own words

> Because the people of Elis were the organizers of the Olympic Games, they had an agreement with the rest of the Greeks that their city was to remain sacred and free from attack; as a result they were complete strangers to war and everything it entails.
>
> Polybios V, 2nd century BC

Greek theatre

Theatre also has its origins in a religious festival, the first drama festival being held in Athens in 534BC as part of the festival City Dionysia. Gradually plays moved away from religion and drama became a separate art in its own right. Some Greek plays have survived and are still performed, for example, The Orestia, Tales from Ovid, The Frogs and Phaedre. At Epidauros in the east of the Peloponnese is the best-preserved Greek theatre. This massive auditorium could seat 14,000 and has become a modern tourist attraction that reminds us of the scale of interest the theatre must have generated.

Dramatic competitions were first held, rather like the Olympic Games, as part of religious festivals. Tragedies and comedies were performed on a flat area called the orchestra, at the base of an amphitheatre. No more than three actors spoke to each other at a time, to avoid confusing the audience and ensure that all actors could be heard. A large group of actors (the chorus), would speak to the audience directly and comment on the play's action. Women were probably not allowed to attend or to take part. The actors wore thick-soled shoes, tall wigs and padded clothes to make themselves bigger and more visible. Happy characters wore bright clothes, while criminals and unlucky characters wore grey, green or blue clothes and those in mourning wore black. Gods and goddesses carried wands and tridents and hunters always carried a purple shawl around their left arm. The actors wore masks made of clay to indicate the character and feelings of the role they were playing. All the masks had large gaping mouths that helped the actors to project their voices. Wigs and false beards were attached to the masks.

In their own words

> *His mother first, being high priestess, now began the kill, and rushed at him. Caressing her cheek he said, 'Mother it is I.'*
> *The Bacchae*, Euripides, 5th century BC

Why you need to know these facts

It is necessary to know what Greek society was like in order to understand the achievements of the Ancient Greeks, and why their civilization still influences the world today.

Vocabulary

Acropolis – centrally located, well-defended area of an Ancient Greek town containing the main religious and civic buildings.
Parthenon – a temple in the Athenian Acropolis, built in the 5th century BC.

Amazing facts

- The Greeks had no sugar but used sweet figs and honey as sweeteners instead.
- Greek words linger in the language of learning today – if a little changed in their meaning. Examples include teacher (*grammatistes*); slave to escort pupils (*paidogogos*); training grounds (*gymnasia*).
- A modern discus weighs about two kilograms. In ancient times it weighed five kilograms.

- The survival of Greek plays is amazing, although given the enormous number of plays that must have been written it is also a matter of some amazement that so few have survived. Thirty-five tragedies by Aeschylus, Sophocles and Euripides, and a few comedies, mainly by Aristophanes, are all that remain.

Teaching ideas

- With the class, stage a mini-Olympics (clothed, of course). You could include events like the standing jump. Have a trumpet to start and stop the races, dig footholds for the runners as starting blocks, add the speeches, poetry readings and dancing that was also part of the Games.

- Using clay, get the children to model the grotesque features of a Greek theatre mask. Once dry, they can use their clay models as a mould for a papier mâché mask.
- Tell the children to write a sports report of the ancient Olympic Games describing the atmosphere as well as the events.
- Read a Greek myth about the actions of the gods to the class. Get the children to tell the story in another form – using ICT, a comic strip, an assembly and so on.
- Women in Ancient Greece had a rough deal by our standards. Tell the children to design a 'women's lib' pamphlet listing all the ways that women were poorly treated and arguing for change.
- Collect pictures of Greek ruins for a display. Have a debate about whether the ruins should be preserved or allowed to decay. (The Acropolis is falling down so this is a real problem.)
- On a large-scale map of the centre of your town or high street, mark in all the architectural references to Greek ideas. You could use a digital camera to make a photographic record, collate the images digitally and add text to make a guide to the Greek legacy in your town.
- As an art project, make a replica Greek vase using papier mâché. Black figure vases had the figures painted on in black whilst the background was left alone. Red figure vases did the reverse. You could simply draw or paint vase scenes using the correct colours.
- Discuss the London 2012 Olympics. Did any of the children go to any of the events? Discuss the similarities and differences

between modern and ancient Olympic sports. Consider the different aspects of running a large-scale event such as the Olympics, and the different jobs that people do to ensure all runs smoothly. Ask the children to imagine they are putting on a large event – what will they need to organise?

Religion and festivals

Subject facts

Religion was a major guiding force for the Ancient Greeks. They had many gods and a great respect for traditions and rites. Respect for traditions was such that Athenian priests were not allowed to bring any innovation into worship and such an act could be punished by death. For example, an animal had to be carefully examined before it was chosen for sacrifice: its skin had to be the right colour; the sacrificial knife had to have a blade of the right shape; the animal's throat had to be cut in a certain way and its meat roasted using the correct type of wood.

The main religion was the worship of ancestors and heroes. By our standards the Greeks were very superstitious – the Spartans would never start an expedition before the full moon, and the Athenian fleet would never sail unless the statue of Pallas was re-gilded. Life was a regular round of sacrifice and worship.

The gods were a kind of family with human traits – gods might covet, lust, and be angry or kind. They lived their own mythological lives and were not always watching what humans were doing. They lived on Mount Olympus, the highest mountain in Greece. The Greeks' relationship with their gods can best be summed up as 'we'll look after you if you'll look after us'.

Festivals were held to please the gods and some were extravagant celebrations. There were festivals to remember the dead, private festivals, agricultural festivals and festivals to celebrate the birthdays of the gods. The big Athenian celebrations were Panathenia (the All-Athens Festival) and City Dionysia. The latter was a theatrical celebration of drama and poetry. Festivals usually included sacrifices to the gods. This was considered a way of making some kind of contact to ask for favours or help. Gods each had their favourite animals, so cows were slaughtered to satisfy Athena and pigs for Demeter.

The main gods on Olympus were:

Aphrodite – goddess of love, beauty and light. Mother of Cupid.

Apollo – responsible for music, hunting and curing disease.

Ares – god of war.

Artemis – goddess of birth, magic and the Moon.

Athena – goddess of Athens and of wisdom.

Demeter – responsible for earth and agriculture; the oldest god.

Hephaistos – responsible for art and craftsmen; blacksmith god.

Hermes – responsible for messages, travellers and good luck.

Hestia – the goddess of hearth and home.

Poseidon – responsible for the sea and earthquakes; Zeus's brother.

Zeus – responsible for thunder, lightning and the weather. Father of many of the other gods and also of legendary heroes. The king of gods.

Other important gods, not on Olympus, were:

Dionysus – god of wine, drugs and dancing (the first plays at festivals were given in his honour).

Hades – king of the underworld.

The oracle at Delphi – consulted by people from all over the Greek world. It was the most important oracle. It was said that Zeus sent two eagles to find the centre of the earth and that they met at Delphi. Alexander the Great is thought to have visited the oracle at Delphi and was told, 'My son, none can resist thee.'

The Ancient Greeks

Why you need to know these facts

Greek religious ideas need to be studied in order to understand the Greeks. Greek religion was also a stimulus for developments that are part of our lives today. For example, the Olympic Games and the modern theatre both have their origins in Greek religious festivals.

Teaching ideas

● Ask each child to design a logo for a chosen god, making sure that it portrays the characteristics that the god would have exhibited.
● Compile a class dictionary of Greek gods.
● Ask the children to write a newspaper report describing festival celebrations in honour of a Greek god.
● As a class, design a web page for the oracle at Delphi, advertising what it has to offer.

The city state

Subject facts

The civilisation of Ancient Greece was based upon the city state, an idea that developed very fast, largely because of the dictates of geography. Small communities, often isolated by the mountainous nature of the landscape and limited usable space, established strong identities. Most Greek cities were no more than 5000 strong in population, although 5th century BC Athens had a voting population of up to 60,000. The democratic ideal was that every citizen had a vote, there were common laws, and a degree of self-sufficiency. Women did not count as citizens and neither did slaves – they had no rights and could not vote.

What were the city states?
Athens was the largest and most densely populated city state. It also tended to be the most powerful, mainly because it had

good access to the sea through the port of Piraeus. Athens was a great coloniser and was interested in trade and sea power. It was also the civilised centre of the Greek world in the 5th century BC and was the centre of great art, literature and thought. Although in 480BC it was destroyed by the Persians, it was rebuilt on a grand scale under its leader Pericles. Athena, goddess of justice and wisdom, was its patron and an owl its symbol.

Sparta was land locked and a more introverted place. Great emphasis was placed upon military prowess, and Spartan boys had an upbringing of legendary harshness. Sparta was ruled by a council of elders, and had an assembly of citizens which took decisions by public acclamation. But its government was not democratic in the Athenian style and was generally marked by rigid authoritarianism. Ultimately, Spartan government was controlled by two kings: they held military power and could overrule the assembly and the council. Fearing no one, their city was unwalled, for according to one Spartan leader, 'It is men, not walls, that make a city.'

Sparta competed for Greek dominance with Athens, although there were times when Sparta and Athens formed an alliance, most notably to defeat the Persian invaders in 480 and 479BC. During the early part of the 4th century BC Sparta was the paramount state, having overshadowed Athens, but its leadership was inept, tyrannical and brutal. Its supremacy was ended with defeat by Thebes in 371BC. After this the Greek states slipped into their old ways of isolation and rivalry until the coming of Philip and Alexander of Macedonia.

Democracy

Athenian democracy in the 5th century BC had at its pinnacle the Assembly, which consisted of all male citizens over 18 years of age that were willing to attend the sessions held every ten days. Whatever the people decided in the Assembly was law. To encourage attendance the state police often did a sweep of the surrounding area and took people along. The system worked partly because the citizens took their responsibilities seriously, and partly because there were checks and controls built into the system. A steering committee of 500 citizens made recommendations as to how the Assembly should vote. Membership of the steering committee or Council was chosen by lot from lists of names nominated by each of the ten electoral districts of Athens.

Warfare

Throughout the Classical period, warfare, or the threat of warfare, was never far away. Either the Greeks were facing the external threat posed by the Persians, or they were involved in internal struggles for dominance of the Greek mainland. Persia had a powerful expanding empire and, under Darius I in the late 5th century BC, tried to conquer Greece. The Greek states were themselves becoming both more powerful and more independently minded, so conflict was inevitable. In 490BC, Darius's army was defeated by the Athenians at the battle of Marathon. But in 481BC his son Xerxes set out with a huge army and navy to avenge his father's defeat. The Spartans faced the Persians at Thermopylae in 480BC. Their army was decimated and Athens was then seized and destroyed. But the Athenians retained their fleet and, with their allies, confronted the Persians just west of Athens at Salamis in the same year. The Athenian naval victory was decisive and the Persians were finally forced to leave Greece for good.

Athens was left all-powerful amongst the Greek states, but sporadic struggles for power continued over the years. In 431BC a huge conflict amongst powerful alliances of Greek cities (led by Athens and Sparta respectively) broke out. It lasted for 30 years and is known as the Peloponnesian War. The pendulum of fortune swung both ways, but Athens' surrender in 404BC was the end of the main conflict.

In their own words

In a night engagement how could anyone know anything for certain? Although there was a bright moon, they saw each other only as men do by moonlight. They could not tell for certain whether they were friends or enemies. After being thrown into disorder, they ended by coming into collision with each other in many parts of the field, friends with friends, and citizens with citizens, and not only terrified one another, but even came to blows. In the pursuit many lost their lives by throwing themselves over the cliffs, for the path down from Epipolae was narrow.

Thucydides, 5th century BC

Why you need to know these facts

The city state was at the heart of Ancient Greece. Much of the civilised development of Greece, particularly the evolution of its political ideas that are with us today, was due to the unique way that the city state developed.

Vocabulary

Hoplite – a heavily armed infantryman in Ancient Greece.

Amazing facts

- Xerxes's expedition to Greece reputedly consisted of over 100,000 men and 1000 ships.
- Greek war galleys called triremes were propelled by oars as well as by sails, and the largest galleys had as many as 150 oarsmen in total. A reinforced prow was used to ram the enemy, but the sides of the galleys were very vulnerable to counter-ramming by the enemy. The Athenian fleet had as many as 300 triremes at one time.
- The combined population of all the city states was probably less than 500,000 – less than most modern cities.

Common misconceptions

Everyone had a vote in ancient Athens and democracy was therefore in its purest form at that time.
In fact this kind of total democracy applied only to an elite. If you were excluded from this elite, by virtue of being a slave or a woman, for example, you had no democratic rights.

The Ancient Greeks

Teaching ideas

- Investigate the meanings of words of Greek origin 'then and now' (start with the list on page 58). How have some meanings changed? Some modern words have a root meaning that is from Ancient Greek, for example *democracy* (rule of the people).
- Tell the class they are to plan a holiday in Greece to visit the ancient sites. Using brochures from travel agents, they should write guides to the sites.
- Explore some Greek discoveries and scientific ideas, such as Archimedes' principle or the sieve of Eratosthenes.
- Establish a 'shadow' democratic government for the running of your class based upon the Athenian model. Tell the children to draw lots for the Council. Will they exclude females? What rules could it make or what issues could it discuss? Try it for a week.

Famous Greeks

Subject facts

Alexander the Great

In the 4th century BC, a vacuum of leadership amongst the Greek states was filled from an unexpected quarter: Macedonia in the north. With the Greek states severely weakened after the Peloponnesian War, Philip II saw his chance to expand his empire. In 338BC, following a decisive victory in the battle at Chaeronea, he seized control of the Greek states. He was assassinated two years later (the finger of suspicion is pointed at Alexander) and Alexander – his son – inherited the new kingdom when he was only 20 years of age.

Alexander eventually earned the title 'Great' due to his astonishing military exploits. He not only dominated Greece but went on to attack the Persian Empire, finally defeating Darius III in a bloody battle at Gaugamela in 331BC. He created a huge empire across Egypt, Afghanistan and Persia, to the borders of India. In 327BC he crossed the Himalayas, but his army was exhausted and his conquests came to an end. He died in 323BC – perhaps of malaria but more likely of poison – in Babylon. He was only 33 years old.

Alexander's greatness tends to rest on his military prowess, which is indisputable. However, some historians think that by the end of his life he was probably an insane alcoholic megalomaniac. Nevertheless, his impact on the Greek world was immense. He took Greek culture and influence to places previously barely known. He also brought back to Greece an enormous amount of information about plants, people, mineral resources, geography and exotic cultures. Many surveyors and 'scientists' accompanied his military expeditions. This Greek intercourse with the East changed the face of the known world, even though his empire collapsed shortly after he died.

In their own words

Be a leader to the Greeks and a despot to the barbarians, look after the former as friends and relatives, and deal with the latter as with beasts or plants.

Advice to the young Alexander
from Aristotle

Other famous Greeks

Aspasia – women were usually uneducated, but Aspasia, the companion of the statesman Pericles, was famed for her intellect and judgment.

Demosthenes – a renowned Greek orator, lawyer and politician. Struggled to rouse the Athenians to the Macedonian danger. Died c.413BC by taking poison after capture by the Macedonians.

Euclid – a Greek mathematician, taught in Alexandria around 300BC. His book *Elements* is a standard work of geometry.

Homer – responsible for the first great works of Greek literature – the *Iliad* and the *Odyssey* – written around the 8th century BC. Nothing is known about Homer himself.

Lycurgus – credited with having created the unique government of Sparta. May be a figure of legend only.

Oedipus – a character in the famous tragedy by Sophocles, King Oedipus unknowingly kills his father and marries his mother.

Pericles – a politician, statesman and general who led Athens during its period of imperial dominance. He introduced payment for people holding public office, rebuilt Athens after its destruction by the Persians, and is responsible for the Parthenon.

Pheidias – an Athenian sculptor whose statues adorn the Acropolis in Athens.

Sappho – a female poet who lived around 600BC on the island of Lesbos near modern Turkey. Her poetry was mainly personal, dealing with her friendships and feuds with other women.

Xenophon – known for his historical writing, but wrote widely on topics from horsemanship to politics. He came from Athens but spent many years in the service of Sparta.

Why you need to know these facts

The achievements of the Ancient Greeks are partly remembered through the work and actions of significant individuals, many of whom influenced not only the ancient world but also the world today.

Amazing facts

- Alexander the Great took his army on a march of 35,400 kilometres (22,000 miles), to Persia, the Caspian Sea, India and Bokhara.
- Alexander killed his best friend Clitus in a drunken rage.

Common misconceptions

Alexander is said to have founded 70 new cities.
This is an exaggeration, but one of his successors, Seleucus, created at least 59.

Teaching ideas

● Make a class presentation on the life of Alexander the Great, explaining why he was called 'Great'. Include a map of his journeys. How many towns were named after him? (There are 11 in Asia Minor and the Middle East alone.)

● With the class, mark on an outline map the travels of Alexander. Calculate the distance he travelled. Can you get close to the estimated 35,400km?

● Ask the children to research what the soldiers in the Greek and Persian armies looked like. Get the children to make recruitment posters for each army.

Resources

The major ancient civilizations are well represented in our national museums and often in local collections too, so check those closest to home before looking further afield.

The British Museum (020 7323 8299, **www.britishmuseum.org**) has been mentioned previously (see page 51) in relation to its collections on ancient civilizations and for the support it offers to teachers. It provides a particularly good site for teachers of this topic: **www.ancientgreece.co.uk**

The Ashmolean Museum in Oxford has a new, purpose-built education centre (01865 278 015) and offers good support for teachers. You can download the KS2 programme as a PDF from the website: **www.ashmolean.org**

Fitzwilliam Museum, Cambridge (01223 332 900) has Greek galleries and, as part of its support for teachers, provides downloadable fact sheets about the Ancient Greeks, on topics ranging from 'Athletics' to 'Women': **www.fitzmuseum.cam.ac.uk**

There will probably be children in your class who have visited Greece itself on holiday and may have first-hand experience of Greek sites to share. You may be able to start a collection of postcards and holiday photographs on Greece. Holiday brochures from travel agents are worth a browse. Photocopiable worksheets have their place; see, for example, *No Fuss Year 6 Photocopiables* by P. J. Noble (Scholastic, 2008).

Books

- *The Usborne Encyclopedia of Ancient Greece* by J. Chisholm (Usborne, 2011) is internet linked and provides a child-friendly, finely illustrated overview.
- *Ancient Greece* by Anne Pearson (Dorling Kindersley, 2010) was written in association with the British Museum, so is a good mix of reliability and quality, and it comes with a CD.
- *Greek Myths* by Ann Turnbull (Walker Books, 2010) has stunning illustrations and is also available as an audio CD.
- *The Orchard Book of Greek Myths* by Geraldine McCaughrean (first published 1992 and still in print) is well written and beautiful. A similar book on Greek Gods and Goddesses is also published in the same series.
- *Tools of the Ancient Greeks* by Kris Bordessa (Nomad Press, 2006).
- *Through Time: Olympics* by Richard Platt (Kingfisher, 2012).
- *Hot Topics: Olympics* by Peter Riley (Scholastic, 2008). An interactive accompanying CD-ROM is also available.
- *Hot Topics: Myths and Legends* by Peter Riley (Scholastic, 2012). An interactive accompanying CD-ROM is also available.

Want to know more?

You can dip into translations of original texts such as Thucydides' *The History of the Peloponnesian War* if you really want to get into the subject. *Ancient Worlds* by Richard Miles (Penguin, 2011), written to accompany a BBC TV series, is a broad sweep but more accessible. A good authoritative source on myths is *Greek Myths* by Lucilla Burn (British Museum Press, 1990). A weighty and copiously illustrated source is *The Ancient Greek World: People and Places* by Nigel Rodgers (Lorenz Books, 2009) and another is *The Cambridge Illustrated History of Ancient Greece* by Paul Cartledge (Cambridge University press, 2002).

The Romans

Before studying the Romans in any depth, it is important to understand that they were the first of a number of foreign invaders who settled in the British Isles in the first millennium AD. This pattern of invasion and settlement largely dictated the unique characters of Wales, Scotland, Ireland and England.

Invasion and settlement

Subject facts

The movement and re-settlement of peoples is a natural process that can be seen continuously in all places across the globe. This intermingling of peoples and cultures has shaped, and continues to shape, Britain today. Generally, invasions take place when:
● the invaders expect to gain something
● the invaders feel that they have a good chance of success.
Ask of the Romans, Saxons or Vikings, 'What did they stand to gain from invasion?', 'Why did they expect to be successful?' and you will begin to discover the underlying reasons for their attacks upon Britain.

Why was Britain invaded?
Britain was a tempting prospect for many invaders. At the time of the Roman conquest, Britain's main attraction lay in its agricultural and mineral wealth. Fertile soils produced rich harvests of wheat. Minerals – such as iron, silver and gold – were not only exported but also worked by Celtic craftsmen into useful and decorative artefacts.

Rome was the most powerful state in the Mediterranean and its well organised army, led by ambitious generals, pushed forward the expansion of the Empire, bringing success, wealth and power. Britain was seized in AD43, during a period of Roman expansion. When the Roman Empire eventually ceased expanding at the end of the 1st century AD barriers (such as Hadrian's Wall) were erected to keep the Barbarians out.

But the Empire did not last forever. Another wave of invaders attacked Britain – Germanic tribes (Anglo-Saxons; see pages 94–113) who were themselves under pressure from the westward movement of people in central Asia. The Western Roman Empire was attacked by Huns and, from about AD440 (some 30 years after the withdrawal of the Roman Legions from Britain) the coastal areas of eastern and southern England were settled by Angles and Saxons. They sought safe and fertile land to set up homes and start new lives. As the defences of Roman Britain weakened, they came in increasing numbers. Over a period of time they came, conquered and settled.

Then, in the 9th and 10th centuries, when western Europe was under attack from Magyars, Saracens and Vikings, Anglo-Saxon Britain became a tempting prize for Viking raiders (see pages 115–31). They shocked the English by sharing out their conquered land, settling on it, and starting to farm.

Each of these successive waves of peoples settled and integrated to some extent with the indigenous population. None wiped out the existing population completely, and all contributed to the cultural and linguistic heritage of the British.

Why you need to know these facts

Understanding our own world is made easier if we see the development of our nation as a continuous process of settlement. In many ways this began with the invasion of the Anglo-Saxons – unlike the Romans they did not pack their bags and leave. But the Roman invasion and settlement marked Britain's first major encounter with the civilised world, and thus is essential to children's understanding.

Introducing the Romans

Subject facts

Who were the Romans?

Rome was originally a tiny village 24 kilometres (15 miles) from the Mediterranean Sea in what is now Italy. It grew slowly, over 1000 years, into a huge cosmopolitan city with a population of about 1 million by the 2nd century AD. From these small beginnings, the Romans created one of the world's greatest empires and eventually, in AD212, granted Roman citizenship to every free person within the borders of the Empire. A Roman citizen might therefore come from Greece or North Africa, and might be black or white skinned.

Timeline	
55BC	Caesar lands in Britain, returns to Gaul for the winter.
54	Caesar lands in Britain again with a larger force, returns to Gaul again to subdue revolt.
AD43	Claudius invades, Caractacus defeated and Colchester entered in triumph.
50	Caractacus captured.
51	Caractacus taken to Rome.
60	Boudica, Queen of the Iceni, revolts.
78	Agricola becomes governor of Britain.
84	Battle of Mons Graupius – Romans defeat the Celts in Scotland.
122	Hadrian visits Britain; the start of the wall.
180	Romans content to retreat behind Hadrian's Wall.
360	Picts and Scots cross the wall and invade.
410	Legions leave to defend Rome.
c.436	Last Roman troops leave.

The Romans

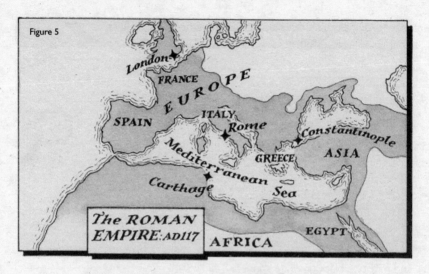

Figure 5

The ROMAN EMPIRE: AD117

How do we know about the Romans?

The Roman legacy is huge and we can find evidence of their lives from sources such as:

● Ancient authors, for example: Apicius (writer of a cookbook); Cato (wrote a book on agriculture); Josephus (a historian); Pliny (prolific writer on all sorts of topics, who wrote an encyclopedia of natural science).

● Legal documents and laws, such as 'The Law Code of Theodosius'.

● Inscriptions – all types, including graffiti.

● Papyri – Rome annexed Egypt in 30BC but it was previously ruled by Macedonian kings, so Roman papyri are mostly written in Greek.

● Archaeological sites – huge amphitheatres, columns, arches and aqueducts still stand, but there are thousands of smaller sites, and many survive in Britain.

What happened to the Romans?

When Rome itself was threatened with attack, the legions stationed in Britain were gradually withdrawn. In AD410, the Emperor Honorius wrote to the provinces of Britain instructing towns to 'look to their own defence', and Roman rule in Britain was effectively over. However, a large Romano-British population remained, and the old Roman town life continued for many years. But as the Saxon raiders started to settle in Britain, a new order replaced the old, and Saxon settlements grew up alongside decaying Roman ones.

Why you need to know these facts

The Romans irrevocably affected the landscape of Britain, the pattern of its roads and of its settlements. We first learn of named people living in these islands through the writing of Romans. Latin, the language of Rome, made a significant contribution to the development of the English language and it was for many years the language of all official documents and the language of educated people. Our language and laws remain peppered with phrases and structures that are Latin.

Amazing facts

The frontiers of the Roman Empire (as shown on Figure 5 on page 80) were defended by over 300,000 men.

The Roman occupation of Britain

Subject facts

Conquering the Celts
Britain was inhabited by tribes of Celts at the time of the Roman invasions. It was situated on the outer fringe of the Empire and was one of the last provinces to be acquired by the Romans.

Julius Caesar had made two invasions of Britain, in 55 and 54BC, but did not stay to conquer. By the time of Emperor Claudius and the final invasion in AD43, trading links with the Empire had already been established.

Cunobelinus (Shakespeare's Cymbeline) had been the most powerful Celtic leader and was friendly to the Romans, but he died in AD40 and his son, Caractacus was anti-Roman. Rome wanted a politically stable Britain, and conquest was one way of ensuring that it got it.

The invasion began when 40,000 men crossed from Boulogne, commanded by Aulus Plautius. The four legions were the IInd Augusta, XIVth Gemina, XXth Valeria Victrix and IXth Hispana. The army soon overcame local resistance and captured Camulodunum (Colchester).

Claudius was lauded in Rome as a great champion and an arch was erected claiming he had defeated 11 kings. In Britain the conquest continued, one army going towards Lincoln, another towards Leicester and a third towards the south-west. The great Celtic hill fort of Maiden Castle near Dorchester was captured, roads and fortresses were built, local tribes disarmed, and any revolt ruthlessly put down.

Resistance to the Roman occupation

Moving westwards and northwards proved difficult for the Roman legions and it took a series of hard campaigns lasting over a decade. The XXth legion, from its forward base in Gloucester, moved into north Wales, but success in battle was not enough to subdue local resistance, as the establishment of forts throughout the west and south shows. The Romans' biggest success came through treachery, when the Queen Cartimandua of the Brigantes handed over Caractacus, the leader of British resistance, to the Romans.

Caractacus

Caractacus (Caradoc) fought for seven years against the Romans and was a major thorn in their side. Unfortunately, opposition against the Romans was never united and the tribes squabbled amongst themselves. Some tried to curry favour with the invaders, and Cartimandua's treachery was probably for this reason. Caractacus' last battle, near Ludlow, was a disastrous defeat. Cartimandua betrayed him, and the following year (AD51) he was taken to Rome to be put on show by the Emperor Claudius. It is thought that he died there about three years later.

Boudica

In AD60, just when Anglesey had been captured and the Romans had at last achieved success in the west, they paid the penalty for arrogance and poor government in the east. Queen Boudica, leader of the Iceni, led a revolt that came within a whisker of success.

The Iceni and the Trinovantians had suffered 20 years of heavy taxation and bullying under the Romans. The veteran soldiers who settled at Camulodunum were particularly aggressive, taking and settling on native land. In AD60 Boudica suffered more humiliation as she was flogged and her daughters were raped. Enough was enough. The tribes rose up under her leadership and attacked Colchester, London and St Albans, slaughtering the Romans they encountered and burning the cities to the ground. They were virtually unopposed until they turned northwards to meet a small force of 10,000 men under the commander Suetonius Paulinus. The huge tribal army was no match for the discipline and military skill of the Roman army. Boudica's force was routed, some 80,000 were killed and Boudica herself is thought to have taken poison rather than be captured.

The Romans took bloody revenge, but they had learned an important lesson and a wiser, more benign regime was installed to govern the area.

Agricola took over the governorship of Britain in AD78 and was the most successful and energetic of the Roman rulers. He completed the conquest of Britain, subduing north Wales and pushing forward northwards to the River Forth by AD80. Many forts were established and the final campaign took the Romans to victory against the British in AD84 at Mons Graupius in north-east Scotland. But the north was never to be fully subdued or settled. By AD100, garrisons had been withdrawn to a defensive position along a line where Hadrian was eventually to build his wall.

In their own words

Each soldier trains every day with all his energy as if in war. It would not be wrong to call their practice sessions bloodless battles and their battles bloody practice sessions.

A History of the Jewish War,
Josephus (AD37–c AD100)

Building Hadrian's Wall

At one time, the idea of building a wall around the Empire would not have been entertained, because the Romans felt invincible and believed that their Empire knew no boundaries. But the world changed. The Emperor Hadrian visited Britain in AD 122 and the construction of the wall began with a view to keeping out the barbarian tribes from the north. The wall was built of stone, although some of it was originally a turf rampart which was later replaced. Except where the landscape provided its own natural defence, a deep ditch was dug on the north side.

It was originally intended to build milecastles along the length of the wall. The scheme was not completed, but 16 auxiliary forts were added. The defensive force on the wall was probably 9,000 men; additional defences were built on the vulnerable coastal fringes at either end of the wall. The legionaries themselves undertook all the building work.

> **Hadrian's Wall:**
> ● defined a military zone where all movement could be controlled (there were ditches behind and in front of the wall)
> ● regulated trade through a few well-guarded gateways, where arms were confiscated and custom duties collected
> ● provided collecting places at the forts for intelligence about unrest beyond the frontier
> ● provided a military base from which attacks could be launched northwards.

For about ten years, up to AD 155, Hadrian's wall took second place to the Antonine Wall, which was about 60 kilometres (37 miles) long and stretched roughly between Glasgow and Edinburgh, 128 kilometres (80 miles) to the north.

Why you need to know these facts

We need to know about the Roman-British conquest to understand how the Romans came to dominate land and people with such relatively small forces.

Vocabulary

Ballista – small Roman catapult firing iron missiles.
Hill fort – a hilltop fortified by ramparts and ditches. Used by the Celts against the Romans.
Onager – a giant catapult used by Roman legions to fire a missile over 400 metres – usually ten of these to a legion.

Amazing facts

● The Emperor Claudius himself led the Roman army in triumph into Camulodunum, accompanied by elephants.
● Hadrian's Wall is one of the engineering wonders of the ancient world, if only because of its sheer size. It ran for 80 Roman miles (73 English miles or 117 kilometres), from Bowness in the west to Wallsend in the east. The wall became the northern boundary of the Roman Empire for 250 years.

Common misconceptions

The British warrior queen was called Boudicea.
Although this is still an accepted rendering of her name, it actually stems from a Victorian misreading of the evidence: Boudicca, Boudica or even Bonduca are preferred. Following the modern trend not to double consonants where there is a choice (for example, focused not focussed), Boudica is gaining the widest currency.

Teaching ideas

● Encourage the children to use the internet to research the Romans. Get them to use this information to create a travel agent's guide to the main Roman tourist attractions, such as Pompeii, Arles, Rome, Cirencester or St Albans.
● Try constructing working models of Roman siege engines, like the **onager** and **ballista**.

● Produce a class timeline showing the main events of the Roman occupation of Britain.

● As a class, make a model of a Roman fort using historical evidence to help accuracy.

● For an assembly, perhaps, produce news and on-the-spot reports of the Roman campaign to conquer Britain. Include a report of the invasion. You could make this an audio experience with background music and sound effects.

Roman society

Subject facts

Towns

The development of towns took time and the first were ramshackle establishments. But the Romans used the town as a way of Romanising the native population. They encouraged tribal leaders to adopt Roman ways and educate their children according to the Roman fashion. Wealthy Romano-Britons were encouraged and helped to establish settlements based near to Roman roads. Some towns were specially planned to accommodate *colonia*, or settlements of retired soldiers. (Colchester was developed as a *colonia* although the site was an old tribal capital.) These places took time to build properly (20 to 25 years) and might have a town hall, a **forum** or market-place, temple, theatre, senate house, comfortable town houses, amphitheatre and sewered streets laid out in a grid plan. Most did not grow beyond 160 hectares (100 acres) in size but they were visible statements of Roman wealth, power and culture, and the natives were attracted by the conveniences of their way of life. London, on a site picked by Roman engineers for its suitability as a trading port, grew to be a centre of administration as well. By AD 100 it was well garrisoned as a provincial capital and became something of a boom town.

Roads

Roads connected the towns of Roman Britain and were essential for trade, the swift movement of troops and the transport of the

Imperial Post. Astonishingly well engineered, their remains are still visible today, and the routes they established are still used. The Imperial Post ran along the principal routes, some 16 routes radiating from London, and had changing stations and rest houses at 19-kilometre (12-mile) intervals. The local area was responsible for keeping the roads in good order.

Villas

Villas were profit-making farms, not luxury holiday homes. They could be small scale and squalid, or extensive and opulent. The richest examples in Britain were the centres of small estates, and these possessed courtyards and verandas with imported marble sculptures and many rooms with painted walls. Like villages or large houses of a later age, villas changed and developed over time, and some became small centres of manufacture specialising in producing cloth or iron tools. Each villa would have had its own slave workers, although evidence of the way they were housed shows that the term 'slave' does not necessarily equate to the oppressed individuals of more recent times. Slavery was a normal part of ancient society; the term was used loosely and could cover people who rose to positions of considerable authority as well as those treated like chattels to be bought and sold.

Most Roman villas were built by wealthy, important natives who adopted the Roman way of life and by Roman immigrants and retired soldiers. They incorporated accommodation for slaves and workers, barns for storage and animals, wells for water and, in the later examples, their own bath houses and central heating.

Baths

In major Roman towns, the streets were laid out in rectangular blocks with a proper drainage system and good water supplies, with public baths and lavatories. Public baths were part of Roman culture and they first appeared in the Roman towns of the south and west of England. Bath still has splendid remains of a system that was part functional, part cultural and part recreational. Individual villas had their own water systems, lavatories and baths, but in Bath we can see the provision at its grandest.

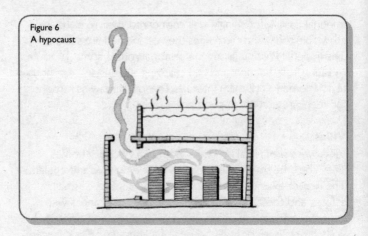

Figure 6
A hypocaust

Baths were constructed with warm and hot rooms and cold plunges to stimulate the body. Many of the baths were richly decorated with mosaic-tiled floors. People found them pleasant places where they could pass an hour or two gossiping, swimming, having massages or playing games. The Romans made sure that they were clean by rubbing oil into their skin and then scraping the dirt and oil mixture off their skin using a blunt scraper called a **strigil**. While in the baths they might use the lavatories, which were sociable places with perhaps 16 people sitting side by side. Additional facilities, such as hairdressers, shops and so on, that we find in modern retail and sport complexes were also provided in the larger baths.

The hottest room was the **caldarium**, heated using an ingenious system called a **hypocaust** (see Figure 6 above), which would bring you out in a heavy sweat, after which you would plunge into the **frigidarium**, with its ice-cold pool. There were drains to take away dirty water from the baths and toilets. Most houses did not have drains, and a pot or bucket served as a toilet.

Religion

The Roman attitude to religion was similar to that of the Greeks: a practical matter; it did not involve much in the way of philosophy or emotion. It was a matter of ritual practices which would yield some benefit – a sort of trade with the gods. The Romans were generally very tolerant about religion, provided it posed no political threat. Native gods and local cults were allowed to co-exist with Roman deities, although the Romans made an exception of the Druids, whom they bloodily persecuted because they perceived them to be a threat to Roman rule. Emperors were, after Augustus (27BC–AD14), given the status of god – generally after their deaths – and a temple was built in Colchester to the Emperor Claudius. The principal gods of the city of Rome itself were Jupiter, Juno and Minerva, and it was the custom to set up altars to Jupiter in the forts established in Britain. There is plentiful evidence in Britain of sacrifices to two popular gods, Mars (a warrior figure) and Mercury (god of trade and travel). After AD312 the Roman Empire was encouraged to become Christian and, as Christianity did not tolerate other gods, it put the other divinities under threat, although the worship of gods such as Mercury persisted for a long time.

In their own words

> *To Jupiter, best and greatest, the first cohort of Spaniards, which is commanded by Gaius Caballius Priscus, tribune.*

An altar inscription at
Maryport, Cumbria

Why you need to know these facts

Life in Roman Britain was unlike anything that had gone before. The first named Briton appears only in the annals of the Roman occupation. To understand what this country was like when it first appears on the pages of recorded history, we must understand the mundane and the ordinary; in short, how people lived their daily lives.

Vocabulary

Basilica – a Roman public hall used for administration. With a double row of columns, aisles down the sides and an apse at one end, this set the pattern for Christian churches.

Caldarium – the hottest room in a Roman bath.

The Romans

Forum – an open rectangular space that was the centre of business in a Roman town. Also a marketplace.
Frigidarium – the coldest room in a Roman bath, containing a cold-water pool.
Hypocaust – the Roman method of providing under-floor heating. Warm air circulated in channels beneath the floor and between walls.
Strigil – a curved scraper used by Romans to clean dirt, sweat and oil from the skin.
Tesserae – small, near-cube-shaped tiles used to make Roman mosaics.

Amazing facts

London (Londinium) covered an area of 130 hectares (0.5 square miles) enclosed by walls, and was the biggest Roman city north of Italy. Modern London is much larger and covers an area of 157,213 hectares (607 square miles).

Teaching ideas

● Every project on the Romans should include a close look at mosaics. There are various ways of making them, depending on available resources and the age of the children. You can make your own clay **tesserae**, fire and glaze them, then set them in plaster of Paris or thistle plaster. The mosaic effect can also be created using coloured squares of paper. Try to be authentic in your choice of colours (usually limited to blue, black, white, yellow and red). The children should study pictures of Roman mosaics carefully before they begin. Concentrate on a small section or examples of the standard geometric patterns that were used.
● Ask the children to try doing some arithmetic using Roman numerals. What happened to zero? Can they find ways of adding and subtracting?
● Teach some Latin. Parts of the *Cambridge Latin Course* (Cambridge University Press) could be used with older pupils,

as it deals with Roman history as well as language. Details on the course and supporting resources can be found here: **www.cambridgescp.com**. Give children some Latin roots to English words (for example, the Latin word *decem* translates to 'ten') and let them trawl a dictionary for words derived from them.

● Make a wax writing tablet. Construct a small wooden frame and use beeswax (melted using a microwave) for an authentic reproduction. Take due care with the hot wax.

Resources

Already in the preceding chapters details have been given of major museums (and their websites) that are wonderful sources of information and teaching material on ancient civilisations (see pages 51 and 75). Most are equally valuable for teachers studying the Romans. For example, from the British Museum you can download slideshows of life in Roman Britain, the Ashmolean Museum, Oxford, offers taught gallery sessions on Roman Britain for primary children and the Museum of London has plenty to offer on the development of Londinium. It is recommended that you browse their websites and those of museums nearby because, unlike the Greeks and the Egyptians, the Romans were an ancient civilization that actually dwelt in these islands; their legacy is all around us. Consequently, there are large numbers of Roman sites in Britain and many museums with specialized Roman displays. So wherever you live in the country, a visit to a Roman site ought not to be out of the question.

You do not have to visit London, Bath or Hadrian's Wall (**www.vindolanda.com**). The Corinium Museum in Cirencester has, as its main focus, Roman Britain and is in a town that still has the remains of an amphitheatre within its boundaries: **www.coriniummuseum.cotswold.gov.uk**. Chester is excellent for Roman remains. Contact the Grosvenor Museum at **www.grosvenormuseum.co.uk**. Details of villas and sites run by English Heritage can be found at **www.english-heritage.org.uk**. Don't overlook reconstructions, such as that at South Shields, where the west gate of a fort has been rebuilt (**www.twmuseums. org.uk/arbeia**) and the Lunt, in Baginton near Coventry, where the timber rampart and granary has also been rebuilt (**www.lunt romanfort.org**).

Ordnance Survey produces maps of Roman Britain, Hadrian's Wall and the Antonine Wall. In conjunction with various museums and trusts and the Royal Commission on Historical Monuments (RCHM), they also produce a number of special local maps, including Londinium and Roman and Medieval Bath. Photocopiable worksheets are widely available; see, for example, *No Fuss: Year 3 Photocopiables*, P. and J. Noble (Scholastic, 2008).

Reenactments

A unique group of enthusiasts reenact Roman military skills: The Ermine Street Guard (**www.erminestreetguard.co.uk**). Their reenactments are very popular. Having been in existence for over 40 years, they are the largest such group in Europe and have performed at major sites in Britain and abroad. They are also the source of much photographic material used in books. Sometimes individuals are available for school visits but their reenactments take place across the country.

Role-play experiences are becoming increasingly popular and are being offered by a growing number of local groups. Check, for example, **www.vitaelampadae.co.uk**.

Books

With so much emphasis being placed upon literacy, it is worth remembering that historical fiction is a useful source of inspiration, a way of appealing to children's imaginations and can provide a good backdrop to a topic. Authors such as Henry Treece, Geoffrey Trease and Rosemary Sutcliff have written good, quality fiction for children. You might start by looking at:
- *The Eagle of the Ninth* by Rosemary Sutcliff – for good readers.
- *Eagle's Honour* by Rosemary Sutcliff (Red Fox, 1995) – contains two stories suitable for most juniors and is available in paperback and digitally.
- *Across the Roman Wall* by Theresa Breslin (A & C Black, 2005).
- *The Stone Street* by Marilyn Tolhurst (A & C Black, 1998).

Here are just a few of the many reference and resource books available that could be useful in the classroom:

- *The Ancient Romans* by Paul Roberts (The British Museum, 2009).
- *Eyewitness: Ancient Rome* by Simon James (Dorling Kindersley, 2011).
- *The Orchard Book of Roman Myths* by Geraldine McCaughrean (Orchard, 2003).
- *Roman Town* by H. M. Martell and M. Bergin (Franklin Watts, 1997).
- *Sightseers: Ancient Rome* by J. Stroud (Kingfisher, 2000).
- *Look Inside: Roman Town* by Alfredo Belli and Conrad Mason (Usborne, 2010) – a sturdy but fun board book.
- *My Story: Roman Invasion* by Jim Eldridge (Scholastic, 2008).
- *Navigators: Ancient Rome* by P. Steele (Kingfisher, 2012).

Want to know more?
- *Running the Roman Home* by A. Croom (The History Press, 2011).
- *Roman Britain* by Patricia Southern (Amberley, 2011).
- *Roman Britain: A Very Short Introduction* by Peter Salway (Oxford, 2000).
- *Life in Roman Britain* by Joan Alcock (The History Press, 2006).
- *Roman Britain* by R. Hobbs and R. Jackson (British Museum Press, 2010) – contains some fine illustrations.

Chapter 6

The Anglo-Saxons

The Anglo-Saxons were one of a number of peoples who invaded and settled in the British Isles in the first millennium AD. It is necessary to understand this pattern of invasion and settlement not least because it largely dictated the unique and different characters of Wales, Scotland, Ireland and England. Before studying the Anglo-Saxons in any depth, it is also important to understand why this invasion was only one of a number that occurred up to the Norman Conquest. Pages 77–8, detail some of the underlying reasons for these invasions, which apply equally to the invasion by the Anglo-Saxons.

Introducing the Anglo-Saxons

Subject facts

Who were the Anglo-Saxons?
The **Angles** and **Saxons** were people of Germanic origin who came to Britain from areas in modern Germany and Denmark. There were many Germanic invaders – Saxons, **Jutes**, Franks, Frisians and Angles (the Mercians, Deirans and Bernicians were all called Saxons by the **Celts**). They were tribal people, closely bound to a group leader to whom they were fiercely loyal. The names of their leaders live on in English place names: Tota's people lived at Tooting, Wocca's at Wokingham, and Haefer's people at Havering.

Timeline	
c.AD410	Romans leave Britain to defend lands of their Empire closer to Rome.
420	Anglo-Saxons build the first houses at Stow, Suffolk.
449	Legends say that Anglo-Saxon leaders Hengist and Horsa arrive in Kent.
563	St Columba establishes a monastery on the Isle of Iona.
577	Battle of Dyrham near Bath. West Saxons conquer the Cotswolds.
597	St Augustine lands in Kent from Rome to convert the English to Christianity.
625	Sutton Hoo burial.
664	Conference at Whitby (Synod of Whitby); decision made to follow the Church of Rome.
731	Bede writes his Ecclesiastical History of the English People.
735	Death of Bede.
789	Vikings land in Dorset.
793	Vikings sack the monastery on Lindisfarne.
865	Great Danish Army attacks England.
871	Alfred becomes King of **Wessex**.
875	Danish kingdom of York established.
878	Alfred accepts the surrender of the Danes.
886	Alfred captures London.
899	Death of Alfred.

How do we know about the Anglo-Saxons?

The Anglo-Saxon period is often regarded as a confused and shadowy period of British history, a time of many kingdoms and little-known kings. Lying between the civilised culture of the Romans and medieval Christendom, it has often been called the **Dark Ages**.

The main reason for this is the dearth of written evidence. What evidence there is comes from documents such as the *Anglo-Saxon Chronicle*, begun in the 800s by the monks of Winchester, which records the successes of the Saxons, but not their defeats. So our main sources are biased against the Celts and Romano-British.

Our main historical sources for this period are:
● Archaeological finds, especially those from Saxon cemeteries and the Sutton Hoo burial site in Suffolk.
● The *Anglo-Saxon Chronicle*, written in English (Latin speakers had all but disappeared by the 9th century). It used the masterly innovation of dating events from the birth of Christ – AD (*Anno Domini*).
● Other written evidence, such as illuminated manuscripts like the *Lindisfarne Gospels*, poems such as *Beowulf* and the *Battle of Maldon*, and Bede's *Ecclesiastical History of the English People*.
● Architecture – there are significant remains of ecclesiastical buildings but no domestic buildings. Archaeology has enabled some reconstruction to take place, such as that at West Stow near Bury St Edmunds.
● Place names (see page 100–1).

What happened to the Anglo-Saxons?

The Anglo-Saxons have never left and Britain is still sometimes referred to as an Anglo-Saxon country. The Anglo-Saxons' impact upon Britain was substantial, not just in language, culture and political geography, but in people. Recent DNA analysis of skeletal remains and comparisons with the DNA of existing inhabitants of Britain have found remarkable links: Celtic and Saxon roots can still be traced. For many people in Britain the answer to the question 'What happened to the Anglo-Saxons?' may therefore be at least partly answered by looking in the mirror. Anglo-Saxon genes may be present in you, as they form part of the racial foundation of many modern Britons.

Eventually the Saxon tribes settled down to live in peace with each other and with the remaining Celtic groups, and became more preoccupied with facing the common threat from the raiding northmen from Scandinavia. But they fought with, and eventually learned to live with, the Vikings, absorbing them into the English nation. The line of Saxon rulers, however, ends with Harold at the Battle of Hastings, and the coming of the Normans in 1066.

Why you need to know these facts

The world of the 21st century is dominated by western culture and is increasingly tied together by the English language, a language that owes a considerable debt to the Anglo-Saxons. The pattern of settlement in England has been substantially dictated by the Saxon invaders and it is still true that most of the inhabitants of these islands, and many who settled in colonies such as America and Australia, are still referred to as 'Anglo-Saxon'. It is a legacy that has endured.

Vocabulary

Angles – in modern geographical terms, invaders from Germany.
Celts – 'Britons' in the context of the Anglo-Saxon invasion of Britain; central and western European tribal peoples in prehistoric and early historic times. Today the term is applied to Irish, Welsh, Scots and Bretons thought of as descendants of these tribes.
Dark Ages – a name sometimes given to the period between the withdrawal of Roman rule and medieval times. The term refers to the lack of written sources from the period.
Jutes – in modern geographical terms, invaders from Jutland.
Saxons – in modern geographical terms, invaders from Germany.
Wessex – literally, the land of the West Saxons, ruled over at one time by Alfred and the centre of resistance to the Viking invaders. Centred on the modern southern counties of Wiltshire, Hampshire and Dorset.

Common misconceptions

That the Anglo-Saxons were Angles (from Angulus between the lands of the Jutes and the Saxons) and Saxons (from what is now called Old Saxony).
Although this is broadly correct, Bede used the term generically to cover all the German invaders. The majority were Angles, Saxons and Jutes; there were also Frisians and possibly some Danes.

The invasion of the Anglo-Saxons

Subject facts

Mercenaries and early raiders

The first Saxons who came to Britain were mercenaries who had been invited by the Roman authorities to protect Britain from invasion by other Saxons. After the Romans left, the hiring of Germanic mercenaries continued, but some of these groups got out of control and started to carve out territory for themselves in the east. Tradition has it that a band of Jutes, led by the brothers Hengist and Horsa, were invited by a British leader called Vortigern in AD449 to help defend his kingdom against the **Picts** (from Scotland). They were given the Isle of Thanet in Kent as a reward, but they revolted and took the whole of Kent for themselves. The date is not certain – and the chroniclers who wrote about these events relied heavily on the writings of Bede, who finished his history in AD731 – but there had been raids before this that the Romans had had to contend with and the Saxon raiders seem to have penetrated far inland by AD 429. But the beginning of settlement, at first it appears by peaceful agreement, was something different.

More and more Saxons from the pagan tribes of western Europe started to come to Britain seeking land, and they began the process of establishing Saxon kingdoms. It is not certain which kingdom came first, but it was probably north of the River Tees, where Saxons had been employed to repel the Picts (from Scotland) and the Scots (from Ireland), that the kingdom of Deira developed.

For more than 100 years the British fought fiercely against the invaders but they were forced to retreat westwards, although, for a time, the Saxon advance was hindered by natural barriers such as the great forest of Selwood, which was 48 kilometres (30 miles) wide. The turning point in this part of English (for that is what the Saxons became) history was the battle at Dyrham, just north of Bath, in AD577, when three British kings were killed and the cause of the Britons fatally damaged.

By the beginning of the 7th century, the Anglo-Saxons controlled most of what we now call England, plus parts of southern Scotland (see Figure 7 below). One group of invaders, by no means the most important or dominant group, eventually gave their name to the country. The Angles gave us *Angle-land*, which later became England.

Saxon kingdoms

At first there were many Saxon kingdoms, but during the 7th century 12 small kingdoms were gradually reduced in number to the three powerful kingdoms of Mercia, Wessex and Northumbria. Offa, king of Mercia, had a dyke dug as a boundary between the English and the Welsh. It ran from the Irish Sea to the Bristol Channel and was 7.6 metres (25 feet) deep and 18 metres (60 feet) wide. The dominance of the Anglo-Saxons in these kingdoms became absolute and today little remains of Celtic (British) place names or words in the English language.

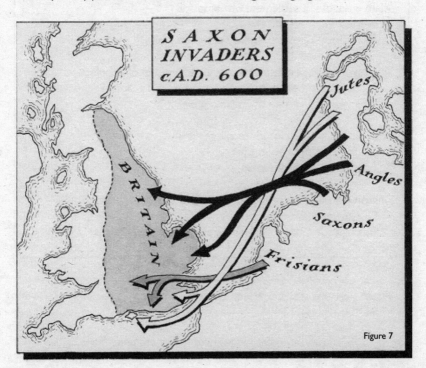

Figure 7

The Anglo-Saxons

Place names

The comprehensive nature of Anglo-Saxon invasion and settlement is clearly set out in the pattern of place names across the UK. Some natural features of the countryside have names of Celtic origin (the Mendips, Ouse, Usk and Exe), but most English place names are Saxon. There are certain endings that indicate Saxon origins. The prefix that accompanies these endings is usually personal, relating to the people whose migration ended there, or geographical, relating to some striking feature of the place.

Some Saxon place names

-ing – this comes from *ingas* and refers to groups of people
| Hastings | Haest's people |
| Reading | Reada's people |

-ham – denotes a settlement or homestead
| Heysham | estate in a wood |
| Horsham | estate where horses are kept |

-ingham – settlement/estate belonging to a group of people
| Nottingham | estate of Snot's people |
| Gillingham | estate of Gylla's people |

-ton or **-tun** – an enclosure or village
| Hutton | farm on a hill |
| Everton | boar farm |

-ington – a village belonging to a group of people
| Donington | farm of the hill dwellers |
| Bickington | farm of Beocca's people |

Why you need to know these facts

The so-called Dark Ages hold the key to understanding the landscape of Britain today. The pattern of settlement, as indicated by place names, provides a major clue to our Anglo-Saxon roots.

Vocabulary

Picts – in modern geographical terms, invaders from Scotland.
Wergeld – in Anglo-Saxon times the price paid for killing a person, a blood price. The more important the person, the higher the price.

Amazing facts

The Saxons called the Britons *Welsh*, which was their word for foreigners. They did not kill all of the Welsh, or push them all into Wales and Cornwall; some co-existed with the Saxons. *Walton* (as in Walton-on-Thames or Walton-on-the-Wolds) means 'Welsh settlement'.

Teaching ideas

● On an outline map of England, get the children to mark with coloured dots place names ending in *-ing, -ton, -ington, -ham,* and *-ingham*. Investigate your local Saxon kingdom.
● On an outline map of Europe, show where the Anglo-Saxon raiders came from. Mark the Saxon shore of Britain and the sites of important Saxon battles.
● Ine, King of Wessex in AD690, produced laws which give us some idea of the value placed on a Welshman, and also show that the Saxons and the Welsh co-existed. **Wergeld** was the compensation to be paid for the taking of a life: for an Englishman it was between 200 and 1200 shillings. For killing a Welshman:

A Welsh slave	50 shillings
A landless Welshman	60 shillings
A Welsh rent-payer	120 shillings

In a class discussion, make a list of all the deductions you can make from this law of Ine about how the Saxons and Welsh treated each other.

Anglo-Saxon society

Subject facts

Life in an Anglo-Saxon village

The Saxons ignored the urban dwellings of the Romano-British and lived, for the most part, in small tribal settlements, closely bound to their leader. They built dwellings almost entirely of wood (their first stone buildings were religious) cut from the forests and woods that surrounded them. They used axes, saws and wedges to prepare the timber for use, and essentially built a house of planks, including planks for a floor with a space below for ventilation to keep the wood dry. Preferably the house faced south to catch the sun; it was roofed using sedge or reeds, and a fire inside would have been contained in a firebox lined with clay. The smoke would have wafted out through gaps between the roof and the eaves (a hole in the roof would have let the rain in and caused a down draught!). Villages were never far from a source of water, for obvious reasons, and everything else they needed came from the countryside around them. Medicines were made from herbs and the land was farmed for food. Surpluses were traded for their other needs such as iron and tools. In many ways the self-sufficiency of the Anglo-Saxon village was little different from the way of life of people in England until the Industrial Revolution. For example, pigs were very important animals because they were efficient providers of food, and this was true right up to Victorian times and, in a few cases, beyond.

Animal bones were used to make small items such as pins and combs (the Saxons were alive with lice and would have needed nit combs), and animal excrement was used for manure. Preservation of food over the winter months was a tricky business, for villagers had to fight with pests as well as with mould and decay. Food was mostly eaten in season, but some was pickled using liquids such as honey. Bread was pretty rough stuff, and grain ground by hand with a quern was sometimes mixed with acorns or seeds to make the flour go further. Almost everything was made at home. Wool was spun by hand and cloth was woven on a wooden-framed loom in the house.

Life was driven by the seasons and the weather, so most of the time people were occupied with the struggle to stay alive. Life expectancy was not very high. But people still found time to make music, to sing and to tell stories in the main hall that served as the centre of every village.

Life and death

Dead Saxons were cremated and their ashes buried in a pot with some personal belongings such as a brooch. Sometimes the pots were decorated with **runes**. As the Saxons became Christian these practices changed and they were buried in consecrated ground without grave goods.

Writing

The Germanic invaders, like the Vikings later, used simple line designs called runes for writing. They also used Roman letters, and the Christian Saxons, such as Bede, used Latin for their manuscripts. The Christian and cultured world of 8th century Britain (the Dark Ages) produced the first writing in Old English.

Beowulf

The longest and most complete poem in Old English is *Beowulf*. It is a great heroic poem and an important historical document. It tells the story of a fiendish half-monster, Grendel, who lives in the fens of Denmark and has killed many warriors. Beowulf sails to Denmark with 14 men to assist him in the fight against the monster. The bloody tale unfolds, and ends with the triumph of the hero. Beowulf becomes king for 50 years, but is killed by a dragon; his body is burned in the Germanic tradition and his men wreak vengeance on the dragon. *Beowulf* was part of the Saxons' oral tradition. It was probably written down when the Anglo-Saxons converted to Christianity (there are several references to the new religion).

Vocabulary

Rune – a letter in the runic alphabet, made from straight lines; these were used to carve inscriptions, usually on stone tablets.

Why you need to know these facts

Learning about the pattern of Anglo-Saxon life is important, not only because it teaches us about the Anglo-Saxons, but also because we learn about a pattern of daily life that continued for ordinary people, with very little change, for a thousand years or more. The beginnings of English, now a key world language, also lie here.

Teaching ideas

● Act out the story of *Beowulf* with sound effects and using extracts from the poem. Alternatively, as a class, create a storyboard, retelling the tale as if for the making of a film.
● Using an appropriate medium, make your own Beowulf.
● The Saxons enjoyed playing with words. Investigate Anglo-Saxon riddles. Encourage the children to make up some of their own.
● Make a class model of an Anglo-Saxon village using information from West Stow: **www.stedmundsbury.gov.uk/weststow**.

Religion

Subject facts

Conversion to Christianity

The Saxons were pagans, and came with their own gods to an island that had been part of the Christian Roman Empire. They sacked Christian churches, but did not impose their gods on the British. We can tell that the Saxons held on to their pagan beliefs for some time, from the pagan burials that reveal grave goods not found in Christian graves.

Celtic Christianity survived, but only on the western fringes of Britain, in Ireland and in monasteries in places like Iona, founded by St Columba. Because, in the end, Christianity triumphed, we have less evidence about the pagan beliefs of the Saxons, although they have a sometimes unnoticed influence upon our culture today. Easter, for example, is named after the goddess Eostre about whom nothing else is known. Pagan winter festivals and fertility beliefs were blended into Christian practices – Easter eggs, yule logs and so on.

In AD597, the same year that St Columba died, St Augustine – a Roman missionary sent by Pope Gregory the Great – landed at Thanet, Kent. His mission was to convert the heathens to Christianity. His tactic was a top-down one: to begin by converting the rulers first, on the principle that the rest of the people would follow. Landing in Kent he sent emissaries to inform King Ethelbert of his arrival and sought an audience.

Politically, Ethelbert may have seen it as a good move to encourage Augustine, but the meeting must also have been an intellectual and theological mismatch: a religion of little theology had to face one whose subtleties had been worked on by the great thinkers of Rome. Ethelbert listened thoughtfully, but he did not overthrow the heathen temples. Instead, he allowed Augustine to repair the Romano-British churches and to preach his message to the people. Augustine was totally dependent upon Ethelbert's support, such that the Kent town of Canterbury remains, to this day, the world centre of the Anglican communion.

Augustine was able to send missionaries around the country, and also arranged to meet the leaders of what was left of the British Church. He demanded that they follow the Roman pattern of worship, in particular that they adopt the same date for Easter. The British Church is said to have taken exception to his authoritarian tone and rejected his overtures. Augustine died around AD604, having become the first Archbishop of Canterbury, but not having managed to spread Christianity far beyond the borders of Kent. Moreover, a rift had been established between the Roman and Celtic traditions.

The spread of Roman Christianity throughout Britain took a century. The conversion of the North and the Midlands was largely due to Celtic missionaries from Iona, so the two traditions of Christianity developed in competition. As various kings gave a Christian lead – notably Oswy, King of Northumbria – Christianity came to dominate the land, but the Celtic-Roman clash remained unresolved. King Oswy convened a meeting at Whitby in AD664 (known as the Synod of Whitby) to settle the matter. The meeting was acrimonious. In the end, the final sticking point was the date of Easter. The King gave his support to the Roman date and the Celtic representatives withdrew disgruntled. The most powerful King in Britain at the time decided the issue: Britain henceforth came within the orbit of Rome, and King Oswy and his wife were able to celebrate Easter on the same date – which, coming from different traditions, they had not been able to do until the decision of the Synod.

In their own words

Our Easter customs are observed in all the world except by the Scots and their obstinate supporters the Picts and British.

Wilfrid, Abbot of Ripon, speaking at the Synod of Whitby, AD664

Monks and nuns

The monastic life was a layman's quest for spiritual purity, and consisted largely of prayer and contemplation. It began with St Benedict, who was born in central Italy around AD500. He eschewed luxuries, like a soft bed and rich food, and withdrew from public life. He eventually organized a community of monks, gave up worldly pleasures, and wrote the *Benedictine Rule* for monks to live by.

The Celtic version of monasticism tended towards the hermit life, which was particularly popular in Ireland. But, encouraged by Pope Gregory, St Augustine made the monastery much more a working establishment, where religious leaders could live alongside monks: clearly the duties of a bishop were incompatible with withdrawal from the world.

Monks and nuns followed the *Rule*. Their basic vows were of obedience, poverty and chastity, and their days were filled with praying, manual labour and reading. With the exception of Sunday, time was spent every day on practical chores, such as growing food, building, cleaning, teaching or caring for the sick. Most significantly, at a time when all books had to be produced by hand, they copied books. Monasteries became centres of learning and some built up great and valuable libraries.

Churches and monasteries

Churches and monasteries were the first Saxon buildings
made of stone, and examples survive to this day (for example,
Brixworth and Earls Barton in Northamptonshire). They must
have been objects of great awe and wonder; in a world where
most buildings were insubstantial and small, these churches, with
their apparent permanence and dominating presence, must have
impressed the common people with the power and wealth of the
Church. They were a visible and constant reminder of their religion.

Monasteries were generally built on a simple rectangular plan
around an open space called the cloister. The sides of the
rectangle were occupied by a church for worship, a refectory for
dining, and a dormitory for sleeping. There were also working
buildings attached, for storing and making things, and there would
also be a library and visitors' rooms. Monasteries appear to
have become very numerous in Saxon times – the diocese of
Worcester alone possessed 30 in the middle of the 9th century –
and they undoubtedly helped to 'civilise' the barbarous Saxons.

By the middle of the 8th century, York had one of the best
libraries in western Europe. These establishments were vital in
carrying forward learning and Christian heritage during a period
of turmoil in the western world.

The Venerable Bede

Bede is the most revered and famous monastic figure of the
period. From the age of seven, Bede was entrusted to the care
of the monks of the Benedictine monastery in Wearmouth
(now Tyne and Wear). Before reaching manhood he went to
an associated house at Jarrow where some 600 monks lived
and worked. Here he had access to a superb library built up by
the abbot Benedict Biscop, and he effectively devoted his life
to writing, producing so many books that he earned the name
venerable (or 'highly respected'). His main work was his *History*,
which took many years of research and is an indispensable
source of information on the Saxon period, without which little
would be known of the men and women who peopled these
islands at that time. It was written in Latin, the language of the
Church, and, of course, is a Saxon Christian view of the period.
Bede completed his *History* in AD731, four years before his death.
He is buried in Durham Cathedral.

St Hilda

The period abounds with Saxon and Celtic saints, and St Hilda was one. In AD657, St Hilda founded the great monastery for men and women (separated, of course, although the clergy were not celibate at this time) at Whitby. As an Abbess related to the King of Northumbria, Hilda wielded considerable influence. She was one of the leaders of the Celtic delegation at the Synod of Whitby, but she accepted the decision of the meeting in favour of Roman rather than Celtic customs. During her life, she became greatly respected and her opinions were sought by leaders of the day.

She encouraged learning and, under her guidance, the monk Caedmon wrote religious poetry in English while at Whitby. (A musical setting of the *Song of Caedmon* is included in the BBC's *Come and Praise*, used widely for primary assemblies.) She died in AD680 aged 66 years.

St Cuthbert

Cuthbert is one Saxon saint whose origins and life are a little unclear. Born in Ireland, or possibly Northumberland, he became a monk because of a vision he saw as a shepherd boy. He attended the Synod of Whitby and later became Prior of Melrose. Next came a similar appointment at Lindisfarne, but Cuthbert craved solitude. He built himself a hermitage on the Farne Islands. For a few years he reluctantly became a bishop in Hexham and Lindisfarne, but eventually returned to his lonely cell on the Farne Islands, where he died. Famous in life, he became even more famous in death, when he was revered and miracles were reported daily at his shrine. The shrine remained in Durham until the Reformation, and superstition dictated that no woman was allowed near it.

Why you need to know these facts

Through the people whom the Saxons thought important – saints in particular – we can begin to understand the beliefs and attitudes of the time.

Vocabulary

Illumination – colourful and often elaborate illustrations, lettering and borders used to decorate manuscripts.
Vellum – a type of writing parchment made from calfskin.

Amazing facts

● Saxon gods gave us some of our day names.: Tiw, the god of battles (Tuesday was Tiw's day); Woden, the god of Sun, sky and war (Wednesday was Woden's day); Thunor, the maker of thunder and lightning (Thursday is Thunor's day); and Frig, goddess of fertility (Friday was Frig's day).
● Bede had no paper to write on. In his time, only the Chinese knew how to make paper. He wrote on **vellum**, the cured skin of a calf. Pen and ink were, like most Saxon utensils, made from naturally occuring materials – quills and fruit dyes.

Teaching ideas

● Examine **illuminated** manuscript designs. Copy an illuminated letter (you may be able to use a photocopy as a template) and get the children to colour it in.
● Tell the children to investigate the life of a monk in Anglo-Saxon times. They should draw up a timetable of his day alongside one showing what they would be doing at the same time.
● The Saxons celebrated many saints. Find out about a few of them. Who in the modern world might we elevate to sainthood? Hold a class debate, and see if the children can agree on just two names for this honour – a man and a woman.

Kings and rulers

Subject facts

The myth of Arthur

It is extremely doubtful whether King Arthur was a real person at all, but in the mists of time and the fog caused by lack of evidence on the early Saxon period, it is inevitable, perhaps, that an heroic figure such as King Arthur should emerge. He is said to have lived in the 6th century and united the British tribes against the invading Saxons. Although the fame of Arthur is widespread, especially on the Celtic fringes and in Brittany, he is not mentioned in the *Anglo-Saxon Chronicle* (see page 96). Myths about the Round Table were introduced at the end of the 12th century.

Sutton Hoo

Because evidence about the early Saxon kings is somewhat shaky, the grave goods from the find at Sutton Hoo in Suffolk are particularly significant. It is thought to be the grave of King Raedwald of the East Angles (or one of his successors) who died around AD625, although no body has been found at the site. The grave goods are held in the British Museum in London, and are both very revealing and challenging. It is by no means clear what all the objects were used for.

Sutton Hoo is near Woodbridge on the River Deben, close to its estuary. In 1938, three low, circular burial mounds were excavated – all had been robbed. When, in 1939, the next and largest mound was opened, a magnificent Anglo-Saxon ship burial was discovered containing objects of enormous value. The finds included a helmet with a realistic face mask, a large shield, a magnificent sword and silver and gold clasps and **buckles**. Enigmatically, there were Christian objects buried in this pagan-style site. The finds had to be hidden in the London Underground for safety during World War II and a thorough examination did not begin until the war was over. The site has been repeatedly excavated, and recent surveys have revealed some 20 low mounds.

The ship, the largest ever found from this period, is about 27 metres long and 4 metres wide. It had been dragged from the River Deben to a hillock 30 metres high, and then placed in a trench and buried. Amidships, a gabled hut had been built to accommodate a very large coffin and the astonishing grave goods. The finds connect King Raedwald with places as far apart as Sweden and Lombardy in Italy, although the strongest connections lie with Sweden.

In only two parts of the world have other ship burials been found: East Suffolk and eastern Sweden. The sword, shield and some other key objects found at the site are also probably Swedish in origin. Many of the objects were locally made, but their design was European. One great silver dish was made in Byzantium; a bronze bowl incised with a camel came from Alexandria in Egypt. Spoons in the grave may have been a christening present.

Although much is speculation, it is clear that connections between Saxon England and the rest of Europe were well established, and that the Dark Ages were not totally devoid of beauty and craftsmanship.

Alfred the Great

King Alfred, King of Wessex, is widely regarded as one of the greatest Saxon kings. He was the youngest son of King Ethelwulf and was born at Wantage in Berkshire in AD853, during a very unsettled period. By the time he had become King of Wessex in AD871, most of England north of the Thames was in Viking hands. But even before becoming king he had defeated the Danes in a battle on the Berkshire Downs. These battles to secure his kingdom were to continue. His successes against the Danish leader, Guthrum, brought a limited period of peace to southern England, until fresh Danish raids in the mid-890s. Alfred died around AD900 and is buried in Winchester Cathedral.

Alfred was essentially a practical man. His law-making mainly consisted of taking the best practice of previous kings and using it wisely. His writings reveal a man who clearly worked to promote the good of the people and who valued learning highly. His story is closely bound up with that of the Vikings, and you will find further information on his exploits in Chapter 7.

Why you need to know these facts

The stories of great figures in history, in particular Anglo-Saxon kings and rulers, are important because they helped to shape the events of their age, but they are particularly important in this period because so little is known about the Dark Ages.

Vocabulary

Buckle – a metal fastening using a pin; remains have been found in grave burials when the material it fastened has rotted. A solid gold buckle was found at Sutton Hoo.
Scabbard – a sheath for a sword.

Common misconceptions

Alfred established trial by jury, divided England into counties and founded the University of Oxford.
He did none of these things. He was perhaps over-lauded by the Victorians, who gave him the title 'Great'.

Teaching ideas

● An ambitious project is to work towards a dramatic reconstruction, perhaps for an assembly, of the Sutton Hoo burial. You could make replica objects based on pictures of the real finds, prepare food for the event, and even make up a ceremony. King Raedwald, the most likely occupant of the grave, had actually converted to Christianity, although the idea of burial with grave goods is pagan.
● Make a 'Book of Kings'. Find out the names of as many Saxon leaders as you can and ask the children to write one entry each.
● Investigate the Alfred Jewel. What was it? Where was it found? Ask the children to write a story about the jewel that could be true. The Alfred Jewel can be seen in the Ashmoleum Museum, Oxford.

Resources

If you live in England there may well be some physical legacy of Anglo-Saxon settlement nearby. It does, of course, depend on where you live but, for example, the town of Wareham in Dorset still has its Saxon turf walls and St Martins, a Saxon church. Do give children contact with something Anglo-Saxon if you can. The major museums are, as usual, worth approaching for both teaching resources and possible visits. A short list of those with particular Anglo-Saxon collections is given below:

● The British Museum in Great Russell Street, London (020 7323 8299; **www.britishmuseum.org/learning.aspx**) – holds the Sutton Hoo treasures.
● Vale and Downland Museum in Wantage, Berkshire (01235 771 447; **www.wantage-museum.com**) – small museum in Alfred's birthplace containing a copy of the Alfred Jewel; has special exhibitions on Alfred the Great.
● The Ashmolean Museum in Oxford (01865 278 002) offers good support for teachers and you can download the KS2 programme as a PDF from the website (**www.ashmolean. org**) – holds the Alfred Jewel and also the jewel found at Minster Lovell near Oxford.
● West Stow Anglo-Saxon Village (**www.stedmundsbury. gov.uk/weststow**) – a splendid reconstructed early Anglo-Saxon village, but more than a static site; excellent resources available.
● Sutton Hoo Burial Mound (**www.nationaltrust.org.uk/ suttonhoo**) – no longer contains the treasures it once protected (those are in The British Museum) but replicas can be seen and there is a splendid reconstruction of the burial chamber on site.

You should certainly investigate place names in your locality for Saxon connections. Seek out a copy of *The Concise Oxford Dictionary of English Place-Names* by E. Ekwall (Oxford University Press), a book that has been through many editions and is still the standard work.

Books

- *The Anglo-Saxons* by R. Loverance (BBC Active, 1992) is child-focused and still available in libraries.
- *Anglo-Saxon Village* by M. Stoppleman (A & C Black, 2000) is an indispensable book about West Stow.
- *Family Life: Saxon Britain* by Peter Hicks (Hodder, 1994) is a fine book with particularly good illustrations.
- *Beowulf: Dragon Slayer* by Rosemary Sutcliff (Red Fox Classics, 2001). The tale is retold for children with dynamic line drawings by the masterful Charles Keeping.

Extracts from translations of original documents can be used selectively with children. The *Anglo-Saxon Chronicle* is such a document and can be downloaded free online from: **www.britannia.com/history/docs**.

The story of the Battle of Maldon is a splendid one and translations of the poem are available. Check here for translations and related material: **www.battleofmaldon.org.uk/links.htm**.

Anglo-Saxon Poetry edited by S. A. J. Bradley (Everyman Paperback, 1995) can still be obtained and contains *Beowulf* and the *Exeter Book* riddles.

Want to know more?

- Oxford University Press have produced *The Anglo-Saxon Age* by John Blair (2002), in their *A Very Short Introduction* series.
- For a general history of invaders and settlers, the popular TV historian is a good read: *A History of Britain: At the Edge of the World? 3000BC – AD1603* by Simon Schama (Bodley Head, 2009).
- Another general read is the more controversial book that also accompanied a TV series: *Britain AD* by Francis Pryor (Harper Perennial, 2005).
- *A Brief History of the Anglo-Saxons* by Geoffrey Hindley (Robinson, 2006) is more tightly focused.

Chapter 7

The Vikings in Britain

In recent years an increasingly cuddly image has been created of the Vikings. Industrious Viking traders, shopkeepers and craftsmen have been shown to have lived in the thriving town of Jorvik (York), and we now celebrate with confidence Viking journeys across Russia, to the Middle East and even to North America. But even though our picture of the Vikings is now more complete, it remains true that they were a fearsome, cruel and heathen people, who extolled warrior virtues and brave death.

The Vikings were one of a number of peoples who invaded and settled in the British Isles in the first millennium AD. This pattern of invasion and settlement largely dictated the unique and different characters of Wales, Scotland, Ireland and England.

Before studying the Vikings in any depth, it is important to understand why this invasion was only one of a number that occurred up to the Norman Conquest in 1066. 'Invasion and settlement' on pages 77–8 details some of the underlying reasons behind these invasions and applies equally to the invasion by the Vikings.

Introducing the Vikings

Subject facts

Who were the Vikings?
The word *Viking* is of uncertain origin but has been applied to all raiders from Scandinavia, whichever land they were from. The raids began in the late 8th century AD when Vikings sailed to England, Ireland, France (Gaul) and the islands of the north on the easterly winds that prevailed in the spring. But from the AD860s Viking

groups started to come to England with their families and were prepared to stay. Many historians believe that in this early period there had been a population explosion in the Viking homelands and that there was not enough good farming land to go round.

The Vikings liked the climate of the British Isles and established winter bases in Britain, some of which became permanent. They started to use horses, and conquered and settled further and further from the sea. The ferocity of their raids built up a momentum that seemed unstoppable until, becoming settlers with homes and families to care for, they lost the advantages of mobility and surprise and became vulnerable themselves.

Timeline	
AD 789	Vikings land on the coast of Dorset.
793	Vikings sack the monastery at Lindisfarne.
865	The Great Army from Denmark invades England.
869	King Edmund of East Anglia killed by the Danes.
871	Alfred the Great becomes King of Wessex.
875	Founding of the Danish Kingdom at Jorvik.
878	Alfred defeats the Danes. Guthrum converts to Christianity.
886	Vikings settle in an area of the country that became known as the **Danelaw**.
899	Death of Alfred.
911	Vikings granted lands in Normandy.
954	End of the Viking kingdom of Jorvik.
960	King Harald Bluetooth of Denmark converts to Christianity.
990	Vikings make renewed attacks and are bribed with **Danegeld**.
1000	Leif Eriksson lands in North America.
1016	Cnut (Canute) becomes king of England, and later of Denmark and Norway.
1066	Last attack by **northmen**, when Harald Hardrada invades northern England and is defeated by King Harold at the Battle of Stamford Bridge.

How do we know about the Vikings?

Evidence of the Viking people comes from a number of sources:

- Sagas (such as the *Vinland Sagas*, written on vellum in the 12th century, 200 years after the events they describe) are an important source, given the lack of written evidence from the Vikings themselves.
- The writings of contemporaries, most of whom were on the receiving end of Viking violence (for example the *Anglo-Saxon Chronicle*). Other writings, such as the *Domesday Book*, also reveal Viking names and habits that were still lingering at that time in the north of England.
- Archaeological evidence (Jorvik, similar settlements in Scandinavia, and L'Anse Aux Meadows in Newfoundland).
- Place names and settlement patterns.

What happened to the Vikings?

Like other raiders and invaders before them, the Vikings eventually became absorbed into, and indistinguishable from, the population of the British Isles. The last true Viking invasion was by the Norwegian, King Harald, who was soundly beaten at the battle of Stamford Bridge by Harold in 1066. But the Normans, who took on the luckless Harold directly after Stamford Bridge and killed him at the Battle of Hastings, were themselves 'northmen' in origin. They had been given part of northern France 150 years previously, following 50 years of repeated attacks.

Norse words and linguistic forms still survive in Britain, particularly in the dialect speech of Yorkshire and Northumberland, in words such as 'lake' and 'play', and in names like Hopkinson and Wilkinson. The Viking language of the Northern Isles of Scotland, called *Norn*, survived until the 18th century, and the Norwegians had a significant influence on Scottish history until the middle of the 15th century. Norwegian law was not abolished in Shetland until 1611.

Why you need to know these facts

Like other invaders before them, the Vikings had a lasting effect upon the places we live in today. Large areas of the country were settled by the Vikings, consequently many place names and settlement sites are Viking in origin. These settlers from northern Europe have influenced the way we govern ourselves, many of our traditions and in particular our language. The Viking *Althing* in Iceland, dating from AD902, was Europe's earliest parliament. Phrases such as 'spread-eagled' and 'bear witness' and even familiar words like 'die' and 'skin', are Viking legacies.

Vocabulary

Danegeld – literally, 'Danish Gold': a bribe, often enormous, paid to the Vikings in order to make them go away. They didn't.
Danelaw – the area of Britain, north-east of a line marked by the A5, where the Vikings were contained at the time of Alfred.

Viking invasion and settlement

Subject facts

Viking raids

The first raid was probably a small skirmish in Dorset, but the best-known early raid was on the monastery at Lindisfarne in AD793, which was vividly recorded in the *Anglo-Saxon Chronicle*, and was clearly viewed with horror by the Saxons because of its sacrilegious nature.

The raids on Britain became more and more frequent until, in AD851, a Viking army overwintered in England. Over the next few years overwintering became more common, and in AD865, so the *Anglo-Saxon Chronicle* tells us, a great army landed in East Anglia and stayed for 14 years whilst being constantly reinforced. The purposes of this army went beyond raiding; it was intent on displacing the Anglo-Saxon kingdoms and their kings. Within 90 years of the first raids, the Vikings had seized Mercia, Northumbria and East Anglia. They consolidated their position in the north by establishing a kingdom based around York that lasted for 80 years, from the mid-ad870s. The *Chronicle* tells us that the Vikings shared out the land of the Northumbrians and then proceeded to plough it and support themselves. Only Wessex, where Alfred was King, stood in their way.

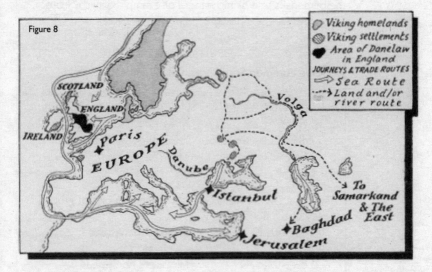

Figure 8

In their own words

On 8th January, the harrying of the heathen miserably destroyed God's church in Lindisfarne by rapine and slaughter.

The *Anglo-Saxon Chronicle*

They came to the church at Lindisfarne, ravaged and pillaged everything and trampled on the holy places. They killed some of the monks, carried some off in chains and, with insults, chased others naked away. Others they drowned in the sea.

Symeon of Durham, writing 100 years later

Places and names

On the face of it, spotting where the Vikings settled from name endings is easy, yet reading the evidence of the past is never quite so simple. It is worth remembering that names coined by the existing inhabitants were sometimes adapted to suit the pronunciation of the newcomers' own language. The Viking *Jorvik* (meaning 'wild boar creek') was originally the Anglo-Saxon *Eoforwic* (meaning 'wild boar settlement'). The Vikings came to Britain speaking Old Norse, which was similar to the Old English spoken by the Saxons (they would still have heard Celtic spoken by some, as well as Latin in the church).

The Vikings in Britain

Many word endings give us a good clue as to the nature of the settlement, but some names are more enigmatic and carry the personal name or nickname. For example, Slingsby from *Sleng* (idler) and *-by* (town or farm).

Some common Scandinavian place name endings:

-by – a settlement, including farms and villages

Coningsby	king's village
Ingleby	village of the English
Normanby	village of the Norsemen
Moreby	farm on the moor

-toft – a Danish word originally meaning 'a plot of ground on which a homestead was built'

Brothertoft	Brothir's homestead
Nortoft	North farm
Lowestoft	Hlothver's homestead

-thwaite or **-with** – a clearing in woodland

Tockwith	Toki's wood
Applethwaite	apple-tree clearing
Braithwaite	broad clearing

-thorpe – a small settlement dependent on a larger one

Kettlethorpe	Ketill's hamlet
Copmanthorpe	hamlet of kaupmenn or merchants
Skinnerthorpe	skinner's hamlet

Why you need to know these facts

The pattern of Viking settlement supplies evidence as to the nature of the invasion, and helps us understand where they settled and why.

> ### Teaching ideas

● On a map of the world, trace journeys made by the Vikings. Ask the children to work out the distances they must have travelled.
● Use an outline map of the United Kingdom to mark places with Scandinavian name-endings. Can the children explain why they appear where they do?
● Eric Thorwaldsson's nickname was Eric the Red and is a typical descriptive Viking name. Other nicknames are Harald Bluetooth, Ragnar Hairy Breeches and Ivar the Boneless. The children will enjoy making up names in the same style.

The Vikings and the Anglo-Saxons

> ### Subject facts

It became common for bribes to be paid to the Vikings in order to keep them from attacking the Saxon kingdoms. This was called Danegeld. But bribery was a solution that did not work for long. The Vikings swept all before them and, the *Anglo-Saxon Chronicle* records, in AD878 an area of Northumbria was shared out by the Vikings, and then half of the army, led by King Guthrum, moved on to attack Mercia and Wessex.

Guthrum was at first successful and surprised King Alfred of Wessex in his winter quarters at Chippenham. Although Alfred suffered a humiliating defeat and was forced to flee into hiding in the marshes of the Somerset levels, he was in a good position to make a comeback. Alfred's dynasty was well-established, there was no conflict for leadership, and he was manifestly a 'good lord' – one that, in Anglo-Saxon culture, is not easily deserted. His return to defeat Guthrum within months was, nevertheless, astonishing.

The Viking army was very mobile. They used horses to move fast (although they always fought on foot), and had the habit of turning up where the Saxons were not. However, the Viking army was now split and diminished in numbers. Alfred had shown previously that they were not invincible. From a fortified headquarters in the virtually impenetrable Somerset marshes at Athelney, Alfred kept in touch with his loyal lords and built up his forces. After seven weeks of guerrilla warfare, he brought his forces together at Edington, near Westbury in Wiltshire, to face the Danes. He won a complete victory; Guthrum and what was left of his army fled back to Chippenham where, after a fortnight's siege, they were forced by hunger and fear into surrendering. Alfred took hostages and insisted that the leaders of the Danish army should be baptized. He first treated them to a feast and demanded that they promise to leave his kingdom.

Alfred set about securing peace. He made arrangements to ensure that half his army was at home while the other half served in the field. He organized the building of new 60-oared ships for his navy that were swifter and higher than the Vikings'. Most significantly of all, he established 29 fortified *burhs*, or boroughs, so that in Wessex no one was more than 32 kilometres, or a day's march, from one.

In AD885, the Danes in East Anglia broke the peace and Alfred retaliated by capturing London. After the campaign of AD886, a formal treaty established the boundary along Watling Street of what became known as the Danelaw. In this area the rule of law was the rule of the Danes, hence 'Danelaw'. Nearly 30 years later, a Viking army was still unable to penetrate Wessex, largely because of Alfred's burghal system.

King Alfred not only secured his kingdom; he earned a position of leadership recognized by all the English in this island. Furthermore, his was not a passive support of learning – he read and acted on his reading, and we know that he ordered his judges either to learn to read or leave office. He also took the offensive against the Vikings by building ships so that he could match them at sea, and he is sometimes called the founder of the British navy. In spite of modern reassessments of his life, the title King Alfred the Great (not one given in his lifetime) seems likely to stick.

By the 10th century, England was united under one Saxon ruler from the royal house of Wessex, but battles against the Vikings continued. Danegeld became more and more expensive to pay and the Saxons more reluctant to pay it. In 1013 the King of Denmark, Sweyn Forkbeard, made a concerted attempt to conquer Britain and his army overran the Saxons under their leader, Ethelred. When Sweyn died, Cnut (Canute) continued the fight with a fresh Danish army. In 1016 Cnut became the King of all England and Denmark. He sent most of his Danish army back to Denmark and effectively ruled as an English king. This was the height of Viking power in England.

Why you need to know these facts

The Viking confrontation with Alfred marked a change in the nature of the Viking invasions. They truly became settlers, and co-existence and integration began.

Amazing facts

● Norwegian Vikings founded Dublin in AD841.
● The Vikings did not only strike westwards from their homelands, they ventured south into the Mediterranean, and then eastwards to what is known today as Turkey (see Figure 8 on page 119).

Common misconceptions

While hiding in the marshes in disguise, Alfred was put to watch over some cakes by an old woman. He let them burn and was chastised.
This story appeared over a century after Alfred's death. Of course, the story could have some foundation in fact, but we have no evidence to support it.

Teaching ideas

● As a class, design the front page of a Saxon/Viking newspaper for the day after the battle of Edington.
● Using maps, a gazetteer and any other sources (such as the internet), ask the children to try to track down the ancient burghs (boroughs) established by Alfred in Wessex.

● Alfred was the only English monarch to have been given the title 'Great'. Do the children think he deserved it? Have a class debate. List all the points for and against his title.

Viking society

Subject facts

Daily life

Excavations, particularly those at Jorvik (York) and Hedeby in Denmark, have thrown considerable light on how Viking urban society operated. Like the Anglo-Saxons, Vikings built their houses of wood, some with walls constructed of wattle and daub, while others (at the end of the first millennium) were constructed over pits nearly two metres deep and had solid plank walls. The roofs were probably thatched.

Food

The Viking diet was built on a staple of bread, although one visitor to Hedeby noted that 'there was little to eat except fish but there was plenty of it'. Wheat and rye were milled together with some wayside seeds, some of which were poisonous, so there must have been a few dodgy stomachs in the Vikings' lifetime. Other common foods and fruits were eaten in season and considerable use was made of herbs to flavour or to hide flavour. Mead, made from fermented honey and water, provided a strong drink. They reared animals; the majority were slaughtered before the onset of winter because of the difficulty of feeding them during the winter months. Vikings ate hares, deer, fish and horse meat.

As with all early societies, very little was wasted. Bones were used for brooches, horns for drinking vessels, skins for clothing. A Viking town had to be self-sufficient: it fired its own pots, made all its own furniture, had its own craftsmen, coin-makers, carpenters, glassblowers and metalworkers.

Clothes

Viking and Saxon men wore similar outfits – trousers and tunics with sleeves. A linen shirt was worn beneath the tunic and a fur or heavy cloth cloak was wrapped around them. They had leather shoes, belts and buckles. Natural dyes made from plants gathered in the countryside produced quite bright colours: blues, purples, greens, yellows and reds. Viking and Saxon women were at first distinguishable because the Vikings wore long pleated dresses with short sleeves, whereas to the Saxon female these were 100 years out of date. They all eventually settled on the loose tunic worn over a long-sleeved dress with their hair covered by a headdress. Amber, jet, silver and gold jewellery was worn extensively by men and women, although gold was rarer and more precious than it is today.

Runes and Sagas

The Vikings had an alphabet, many to be precise, formed from runic letters, which were made up of straight lines. They had no paper, so the **runes** were mostly carved as inscriptions on stones and memorials, hence the need for straight lines. Although knowing the runes was prized as an almost magical skill, the runic legacy does not form an extensive literature. They are simple records of deeds, memorials to the dead, and sometimes mere graffiti.

The most extensive written record, written on vellum long after the events they describe, were the sagas begun in the 12th century. The Vikings had a strong oral tradition and stories of great deeds were handed down by word of mouth, but eventually came to be written down. The sagas are written in a simple, direct style and are often bloodthirsty. *Njal's Saga*, for example, describes a 50-year blood feud. The *Vinland* (Wineland) *Sagas* tell of Erik the Red's founding of a colony in Greenland and of the discovery of North America by **Norsemen** 500 years before Columbus.

In their own words

> Njal's sons had many enemies. Flosi gathered them together and rode to Njal's farm. They surrounded it and set it on fire. When Njal saw there was no escape, he went to bed to die quietly.
>
> *Njal's Saga*

Warriors

Warriors were the most important people in Viking society. At 12 years of age, a Viking boy legally became an adult and would be taken on raids. To be a warrior was the highest ambition. A Viking's weapons were his most precious possessions, and were given names such as Legbiter (a sword), Battle Wall (a shield) and Battle Rain (arrows). Viking warriors wore metal helmets but little other protective armour except leather jerkins. A chief might afford a tunic of chain mail.

Most feared of all the Viking warriors were the **berserkers**, named after the 'bearskins' or 'bare skins' (we are not sure which) that they sported. These warriors fought in a kind of hypnotic rage that may have been drug-induced. They were respected but also feared by other Vikings. Warriors of the great raiding parties that stayed in England were almost certainly professional soldiers who lived from the spoils of war.

Viking society comprised three main groups. At the top were the lords or aristocracy, called **jarls**. They were warriors and leaders who were expected to lead by example and not to be outdone by the valour of their men. At the bottom were those in effective slavery, called **thralls**. In the middle of this social sandwich was the largest group, known as **karls**. These included craftsmen, traders and farmers; all the 'middle class' as it were. They were also the warriors who went off to war, leaving their houses and land in the care of the womenfolk.

In their own words

> Berserkers were men helped by **Odin** in battle. They refused to wear byrnies and fought like wolves or mad dogs. They began by biting their shield rims, then they cut down the enemy, and neither fire or iron could stop them.
>
> Ynglinga Saga

Ships

The Vikings would not have got anywhere without their ships and their famed seafaring ability. Not all Viking ships were the same; it is clear from the substantial finds preserved in the cold water and thick clay of Scandinavia that different ships were built for different purposes. There were cargo ships, merchant ships (called **knörr**), fishing vessels and **longships** or warships (sometimes called 'dragon ships' because of the decorated dragon's heads that were often carved on the **prow**). The latter could be up to 55 metres long. The longship preserved in Gokstad in Norway is 23 metres long.

Overlapping planking fastened together with clenched nails (iron rivets) provided the outer skin of the boat, a method of construction called 'clinker'. Gaps between the boards were caulked with moss and tarred wool to make them watertight. At the stern of the ship was the steerboard, used as a crude rudder. A sturdy oak keel provided the ship's backbone, although it was not a true keel, being wider than it was deep. The draught of the ship was shallow, only two to three metres. The bottom of a longship was flat which allowed it to sail in shallow water. It was reasonably light so that it could be dragged over land on wooden rollers. As a result of their advances in ship design, Vikings were able to sail further and faster than any before them.

A single sail and oars propelled the ships across the North Sea. Each oarsman had his own space, which was called a 'room'. Personal possessions would be kept in a chest on which they sat, but all sorts of general provisions – such as water barrels, grain, weapons and even animals – were also stored on board.

Why you need to know these facts

We cannot understand the Vikings properly without understanding something about the sorts of daily lives that they led.

Vocabulary

Berserker – a Viking warrior who fought in a wild rage.
Byrnie – a Viking warrior's protective jerkin, often made of leather.
Jarl – a person in the highest order of Viking society; a lord, warrior and leader.
Karl – a person in the middle order of Viking society; perhaps a craftsman or farmer, as well as a warrior.
Kenning – a figure of speech used to give a descriptive, and often poetic, name for something, for example 'whale road' for the sea (from Beowulf).
Knörr – a Viking cargo ship.

Longship – the shallow-drafted ships, pointed at both ends, which carried the Vikings on their raids to Britain.
Norseman – another name for a Viking.
Odin – chief of all the Viking gods, responsible for war and wisdom.
Prow – the front of the ship; usually adorned with a fierce dragon's head or similar on Viking war vessels.
Rune – a letter in the runic alphabet, made from straight lines; these were used to carve inscriptions, usually on stone tablets.
Thrall – a person in the lowest order of Viking society, who would have lived in bondage to a master.

Amazing facts

It is thought that berserkers chewed poisonous toadstools (*fly agaric*) to bring on their wild behaviour.

Common misconceptions

Vikings wore horned helmets.
This belief has no foundation in evidence, in spite of the fact that Hollywood films have regularly portrayed Vikings in this way. The horned helmet is, rather strangely, used as a symbol of Danish national identity and is worn by crowds at major sporting events, such as the Olympic Games or the World Cup.

Teaching ideas

● Ask the children to research a runic alphabet and write a short message in runes.
● Make up a story in the style of a saga. It should be told, not written. Try asking some children to retell the story with embellishments. Can they remember it? Could the children sit in a circle and each tell a part of the story, made up as they go along? Less confident children could be given prompts for topics by the teacher.

- The Vikings enjoyed using *kennings*: phrases like 'the ship of the ground' to describe a horse. Get the children to create kennings to describe key features of your school (people included).
- Make models of Viking ships. The class could test them using a water tray and a small fan. Can they design one that will float and sail without toppling?
- The Vikings loved designs with intertwining motifs. Search for examples and create a class Viking design book. Use the internet to gather more information.
- With the children, invent a dance or mime based on the actions of berserkers.
- Using the information gained in the research above, children in the role of Vikings could give short talks about their lives, or be interviewed for a fictitious (and anachronistic!) radio programme.
- Dress up two children, one male and one female, as accurately as you can as citizens of Jorvik.
- The children could make and decorate (in card) a replica Viking sword based upon existing archaeological remains.

Viking beliefs and deities

Subject facts

People living near the coasts of Britain and Europe were in dread of the Vikings partly because, being heathens, they had no respect for the Church. They were also ferocious warriors because their culture extolled the virtues of a brave death. Ironically, a brave opponent could also be honoured, when captured, by being put to death in an excruciatingly painful way as a celebration of his bravery.

Viking gods were also without mercy and focused on courage and death. Dying in battle was a high honour because you were taken straight to **Valhalla** (the hall of the chosen or slain), which was a sort of warrior heaven, accompanied by warrior maidens called **Valkyries**. In this warrior heaven, ruled over by *Odin*, the god of wisdom and war, warriors would fight all day and feast all night.

Thor (the god of thunder and justice) rode in a chariot pulled by two goats and carried a hammer, which was the symbol for lightning. He was the most popular god with ordinary people – hence the many lucky charms that have been found in the shape of a hammer. Vikings believed that Thor protected them from cold, hunger, giants and many other dangers. He was not clever but was immensely strong, and defended **Asgard** against any powers that threatened the Viking heaven. The word 'Thursday' comes from his name (see page 109).

Viking gods and goddesses belonged to two groups, called the *Aesir* and the *Vanir*. The Aesir was the larger family; at its head was Odin, the 'all-father'. Odin was the war chief, a sinister god who demanded sacrifices (these could, on occasion, be human). Victims were slaughtered to ask for victory and to celebrate it. Odin had only one eye – he lost the other in a search for knowledge. He rode on a horse with eight legs and on his shoulders stood two ravens, Hugin (memory) and Munin (mind). They flew into the world to find out what was going on and whispered information in his ears. Odin was a very complicated god and the beliefs that surrounded him were connected with sorcery and evil. **Frigg** was married to Odin and she was the queen of the Viking gods.

Frey (the god of harvest) was the third great Norse deity. He belonged to the smaller family of gods, the Vanir, and was the farming god. His wife, **Freya**, was the goddess of love and beauty. She travelled through the sky in a chariot drawn by two cats.

The Vikings and Christianity

Contact with Britain and the rest of Europe brought the Vikings into contact with Christianity, a religion that they were not slow in taking up. Vikings were converted in their homelands; King Harald Bluetooth of Denmark was one of the first to convert, in AD960. In a typically Viking act, when a Viking king in Kiev became a Christian, he forced all his subjects into the River Dnieper to be baptized. When King Alfred defeated Guthrum, Guthrum too converted to Christianity. But there was a clear period when Christian and pagan beliefs co-existed. A degree of expediency may have accelerated Viking conversions because they were great traders, and most of their trading was carried out across a largely Christian world.

Why you need to know these facts

Although Viking religion was superseded by Christianity, there are still cultural throwbacks to their pagan beliefs lingering in Western society today – the music of Wagner, for example.

Vocabulary

Asgard – the 'heaven' inhabited by the Viking gods, containing Valhalla.
Frey – Viking god of harvest.
Freya – Viking goddess of love and beauty.
Frigg – queen of the Viking gods; Odin's wife.
Sleipnir – the eight-legged horse ridden by the chief of the Viking gods, Odin.
Thor – Viking god of thunder and justice.
Valhalla – the great palace in the Viking warrior's heaven.
Valkyrie – maidens who brought Viking warriors killed in battle to Valhalla.

Teaching ideas

- Paint pictures to adorn the mythical hall of the dead, Valhalla. Play the *Ride of the Valkyries*, by Wagner, as inspiration.
- Thor's symbol was a hammer. The children could design a lucky charm or brooch that might have been worn by a Viking as a symbol of this god.
- In a class discussion, list all the reasons that the children can think of why the Vikings discarded their gods in favour of the Christian one.

Resources

A trip with your class over the sea to Sweden or Denmark to visit the relevant museums in the Viking homelands might just be beyond your school budget, but there are museums in Britain that contain collections worth viewing. Museum details have been given in previous chapters and there is clearly some overlap between Saxon and Viking material, so check out the contacts given.

Jorvik Viking Centre in York, is the key place to go for Viking artefacts, Viking displays, support for teachers and 'Viking' experiences. It is a stimulating place; a little 'showbiz' in its approach but can provide a good day out (including smells!): 01904 615 505; **www.jorvik-viking-centre.co.uk**.

Regia Anglorum is a society dedicated to reenactments of British History, especially Anglo-Saxon and Viking. They claim they are possibly the largest 'living history' society in the world. It is worth checking on their programme of events to see whether there is one near you: **www.regia.org**.

Books
This is a popular subject, perhaps because it lends itself to dramatic illustration, so new books are appearing all the time. Here are few, old and new, to start with:

- *Myths of the Norsemen* by Roger Lancelyn Green (Puffin, 1994) – has been described as containing a seam of 'bone-chilling cold'.
- *Faber Book of Northern Legends* by K. Crossley-Holland (Faber, 1983) – first published over 20 years ago but worth tracking down a library copy.
- *My Story: Viking Blood* by Andrew Donkin (Scholastic, 2008) – fiction in a period context.
- *Eyewitness: Viking* by Susan Margeson (Dorling Kindersley, 2008) – a vividly illustrated resource using a well-tested publishing formula.
- *Viking World* by P. Wingate and A. Millard (Usborne, 2008) – accessible information in an internet-linked volume.

- *Vikings* by P. Wilkinson (Carlton, 2008) – a large, sturdy board book including pop-ups.
- *Usborne Beginners: Vikings* by S. Turnbull (Usborne, 2006) – a simple but useful book.
- *Hot Topics: Myths and Legends* by Peter Riley (Scholastic, 2012) – has a chapter on the Vikings; an accompanying interactive CD-ROM is also available.

Want to know more?

In Oxford University Press's *A Very Short Introduction* series there is *The Vikings* by Julian D. Richards (Oxford University Press, 2005). It is very short.

The Aztecs

Do you think of pumping hearts being ripped from human chests by half-naked priests armed with sharp stone knives when you think of the Aztecs? This vivid image may be the one that sticks in the mind, but there was much more to the Aztecs than bloody sacrifice.

Though warlike and callous by our standards, the Aztecs had enormous creative energy and produced well-ordered towns, pyramid temples, palaces and marketplaces – in fact, the most sophisticated civilisation that Central America had ever known.

Introducing the Aztecs

Subject facts

Who were the Aztecs?

The name *Aztec* describes the group of people, mainly the Mexica and Acolhua, whose empire dominated Central America in the 15th century AD.

The Valley of Mexico was the heart of the Aztec Empire. It is surrounded by volcanic mountains but has rich, deep soil and many shallow salty lakes. An island in the central lake, Lake **Tetzcoco**, was the site of the Aztec capital. The rest of central Mexico is mountainous, with steep wooded slopes, so most people lived in the large highland valleys.

The Aztec Empire lasted from AD1428 to 1521. This is the classic Aztec period when their culture flourished and dominated Central America. But the roots of the Aztec civilization go back much further, to the nomadic Mexica tribe living in the northern

desert. These **Nahuatl**-speaking people migrated south around
AD 1150, and over the next 200 years a series of city states
were founded.

Once the Mexica had settled in these areas, where there were
abundant and rich food supplies, the population grew rapidly.
Swamp delicacies (cakes made out of algae, fish, turtles, salt and
insect larvae) were exchanged for building materials and other
desirable commodities. The Aztecs were fierce warriors so they
gradually became both rich and powerful. Their domination was
finally asserted in a series of alliances and conquests.

Timeline	
c.AD 1150	*Migration of the nomadic Mexica tribe southwards to Central America.*
1200	*Nomadic Aztec tribe reaches the Valley of Mexico claiming to be descendants of the warlike Toltecs.*
1325	*Aztecs establish their great city of Tenochtitlan on a swampy island in Lake Tetzcoco.*
1428–1519	*The 'Triple Alliance Empire' – the height of Aztec civilization.*
February 1519	*Spanish military leader Hernán Cortés sets sail from Cuba with an army of 500 and 11 ships to explore the coast of Mexico. On landing in Mexico, Cortés is greeted by messengers from the Aztec king, Moctezuma II.*
November 1519	*Cortés enters Tenochtitlan. Fighting breaks out in the capital between the Spanish and the Aztecs. Moctezuma dies, possibly killed by a stone thrown by one of his own people.*
30 June 1520	*Noche triste (the night of sorrows). The Spanish fight their way out of the capital taking many casualties.*
1521	*Fall of Tenochtitlan, the Aztec capital, to the combined forces of the Spanish and the Cholollan and Tlaxcalan Indians. End of the Aztec Empire.*
1521–48	*Typhus and other diseases kill 60 per cent of the Aztec population.*

The Aztecs

Figure 9 shows southern Mexico and the Central American states today. The shaded area shows the extent of the Aztec Empire just before its collapse in 1521. Archaeologists refer to this area as *Mesoamerica*.

After the conquest of the Aztec Empire, Spanish gradually replaced Nahuatl as the main language spoken, and by the beginning of the 20th century most, if not all, Mexicans were of partial Spanish ancestry.

How do we know about the Aztecs?

Native pictorial manuscripts provide a limited amount of information. The Aztec pictorial writing system could not record the spoken word fully, only a limited range of names and ideas. These 'pictures' were used to jog the memory of the reader who would then fill in the detail from his own knowledge. The manuscripts (called **codices**) were written on paper made from the inner bark of the wild fig tree or deerskin. Only a few survive from before the Spanish conquest, although they continued to be painted for generations after the end of the Empire.

Several of the conquerors wrote reports of their deeds. Cortés himself and Diaz del Castillo wrote at length, but they give an account from the Spanish viewpoint only.

The years following the conquest were extensively chronicled by Spanish priests (Friar Diego Durán – see page 148 – and

Friar Bernardino de Sahagun made systematic records of Aztec culture). Ixtlilxochitl and Chimalpahin wrote two particularly important chronicles; both writers were descendants of Aztec nobles.

Archaeology, especially when aided by modern technology, continues to yield information about the Aztec past. Many Aztec sites lie under Mexico City.

What happened to the Aztecs?

The end of the Aztec Empire was precipitated by the Spanish invasion in 1521. Attracted by tales of an amazing civilization, rich beyond measure, and fired by religious conviction that is hard for some to understand today, an army of Spanish adventurers (usually referred to as **conquistadores**) under Hernán Cortés set out to explore the region. They were welcomed at first, albeit warily, by the Aztecs, and invited into the capital Tenochtitlan by Moctezuma, the emperor.

The Spanish were in Tenochtitlan for two weeks as guests, but they soon realized that they were virtual prisoners. They seized Moctezuma as a hostage and held him for several months, but the city began to seethe with unrest. The emperor tried appeasement, and even built a Christian shrine on the steps of the great pyramid as a concession to the Spaniards. Moctezuma warned Cortés that he could not control his people and told the Spanish to leave for their own safety. The Spaniards killed some Aztec lords and the Aztecs attacked, seeking vengeance; the emperor was called upon to calm his people but, according to Spanish accounts, he was stoned by them and died. Native historians later claimed that the Spanish strangled him. The truth is uncertain.

After being forced to beat a hasty retreat from Tenochtitlan at night and with many casualties, the small Spanish army, combined with thousands of opportunist Chololan and Tlaxcalan Indians, returned to lay siege to the city.

Superior tactics and weapons (the Aztecs had no firearms), combined with the decimating effect of starvation, disease and the lack of fresh water, eventually led to the fall of the city in August 1521. During the final attack, wholesale slaughter was carried out by the Tlaxcalans on their former oppressors, with a ferocity that shocked even the battle-hardened Spanish. In the confusion, the last emperor, Cuauhtemoc, was captured as he tried to escape. His surrender was accepted by Cortés himself, who treated him honourably. A quarter of a million Aztecs in Tenochtitlan were overcome by a force of no more than 900 Spaniards and several thousand Indian allies.

Having defeated the Aztecs, the Spanish set about systematically converting the Indian population to Christianity. Spanish priests arrived who learned the Nahuatl language to speed up the conversion process; they sometimes carried out mass baptisms. Aztec temples were razed to the ground and Christian churches were built on top of some of the largest pyramids. Alongside this religious conversion, a feudal system of tribute and labour was used to control the conquered. But more significantly and dramatically, the native population was also reduced by disease to little more than a tenth of its former size within 40 years (the best estimate of Aztec numbers in the years immediately preceding the conquest is 920,000). The Spanish stripped the country of its gold and silver, melted down the sacred objects and shipped most of the treasure back to Spain. (Divers still retrieve treasure from the ships that sank en route to Europe.)

In their own words

Like monkeys they seized upon the gold. For in truth they thirsted mightily for gold; they stuffed themselves with it, and starved and lusted for it like pigs.

The words of a native observer describing Spanish reactions to the gifts offered to them by Aztec ambassadors.

Why you need to know these facts

The Aztecs established the largest and most remarkable empire in Mesoamerican history and their creative achievements, particularly in civic organisation, are impressive. But the fall of the Aztec Empire marked a major turning point in American history and permanently changed the culture of the region. Pre-Hispanic heritage still profoundly affects Mexico, and is critically important to our understanding of modern America.

Codice – manuscripts of Aztec 'glyph' writing.
Conquistadores – 'conquerors' in Spanish; the adventurer-soldiers of the 16th-century Spanish Empire.
Nahuatl – the language spoken by the majority of Aztecs.
Tetzcoco – the lake and swamp where the Aztec capital Tenochtitlan was built. (Common alternative spelling is 'Texcoco'.)

Amazing facts

- Nahuatl is one of 50 languages still spoken in Mexico today.
- A series of epidemics – chiefly measles, typhus and smallpox – wiped out most of the Aztecs. These diseases were brought to the new world by Spanish conquistadores and the native population had no resistance to them. The biggest killer was typhus, which killed an estimated 60 per cent of the Aztec population in the period between 1521 and 1548.

Aztec society

Subject facts

The soil really was the Aztec lifeblood, and their lives revolved around the demands of farming – planting, weeding, winnowing and storing grain. The soil was used to sustain life and also to give pleasure – the rich created wonderful gardens that greatly impressed the first Europeans to see them.

Diet

The Aztec diet was basically vegetarian – maize was eaten in large quantities. Meat from hunted animals formed a minor part of the diet, which was supplemented by beans, the prickly pear cactus, and the widespread consumption of insects including ants, grasshoppers, maguey worms and larvae. Chillies provided

Vitamin C, and the Aztecs also ate squashes, calabashes, tomatoes and sweet potatoes. Maguey (an agave plant similar in appearance to aloe) and cotton were grown to provide fibre for weaving.

Social structure

Aztec society was divided into nobles and commoners, and there was a wide gap between them. Although the nobles were greatly outnumbered, they owned most of the land, commanded the army, and lived lives of luxury. Commoners owed some duties to both kings and nobles but managed to live much of their lives without undue interference. The nobles both lived and worked in their large palaces.

Growing up

Between the ages of 10 and 20 all boys and girls attended schools. They received training in singing, dancing and playing musical instruments. Boys were taught separately from girls and the main elements in their curriculum were martial arts and military training. Children of promising commoners were taught the arts and military, religious and astrological knowledge, alongside the children of nobles in special schools.

Men married in their early twenties and girls were often married as early as ten or twelve years of age.

The arts

Amongst other activities the Aztecs derived pleasure from dancing and singing. Most of this was done at ritual and ceremonial occasions – we do the same at weddings and birthdays. The dances were rhythmically strong and involved chanting. Some were sober and formal, but the 'dances of youth' were flirtatious and exciting. Spanish priests thought that the Aztec 'wriggling and face pulling' in these dances was highly improper and immoral.

Pottery flutes, rattles and trumpets made from cut conch shells were used in music-making, as were wooden gongs. Feather bundles and rattles featured in most dances.

Skill in performing hymns and poetry was greatly admired, as was public oratory – perhaps not surprising in a culture that lacked a subtle written language.

Stone was a major medium for sculpture and animals were the most frequent subject, particularly snakes and the highly important jaguar. The jaguar was a symbol of power and strength, and carvers produced many small ritual objects depicting it. Art, as in all early societies, was functional – the concept of 'art for art's sake' was unheard of. Painting used ritual symbols, such as a feathered serpent and standardized geometric images. Strong black outlines were combined with bright, flat colours and exaggerated main features to produce a clear, distinctive style.

Aztec hieroglyphs

Aztec picture-writing was a bit like modern logos or coats of arms, in that the signs and symbols always told a story. For example, the place names Tochtepec and Tzonpanco meant 'on the hill of the rabbit' and 'on the skull rack' respectively – their hieroglyphs are shown in Figure 10.

Figure 10

TOCHTEPEC   TZONPANCO

In their own words

There are very refreshing gardens with many trees and sweet-scented flowers and bathing places of fresh water. Within the orchard is a great pool of fresh water with sides of handsome masonry and a well-laid pavement of tiles. The pool contains many different kinds of fish and waterfowl. There are hedges of latticework made of cane behind which are plantations of all sorts of trees and aromatic herbs.

Hernán Cortés describing the palace garden
of Cuitlahuac in a letter to Charles V, 1520,

Why you need to know these facts

Knowledge about the quality of life in Aztec times is necessary in order to understand why many consider the Aztecs to have been 'civilised'. Blood sacrifices need to be seen against a backdrop of an organised and impressive culture.

Amazing facts

● Cornflakes are made from maize, which was a staple of the Aztec diet. Do you start the day the Aztec way?
● The Aztecs did not use money. Most trade was by barter, but cacao beans were used as a kind of currency.
● The Aztecs chewed gum (chicle and bitumen) to clean their teeth.

Common misconceptions

The Aztecs were cannibals.
Not strictly true. Although human flesh was sometimes consumed by warriors as part of religious ceremonies, the Aztecs did not eat human beings as part of their staple diet.

Teaching ideas

● Examine some familiar modern 'glyphs', such as the badge of Arsenal Football Club or your county or city coat of arms. Explain what the pictures mean.
● Create an Aztec-type hieroglyph to represent your school, home, street or village.
● Investigate Aztec art by choosing an example to copy. There are some famous turquoise mosaic masks in the British Museum that you could reconstruct using clay or Plasticine®. Use this clay or Plasticine® model as a mould to create a papier-mâché mask, complete with coloured paper and an extra layer of PVA adhesive for a glossy effect.

Religion

The central idea of Aztec religion was that of sacrifice. The Aztecs believed in many gods who sacrificed themselves for the benefit of mankind: in one myth the gods threw themselves on a huge fire to create the Sun.

Creation myth

Creation myths are common to most religions and the Aztec religion is no exception. In the beginning there was a high god called Ometeotl (the name means 'two-god' because there was both male and female in him). This 'two-god' produced four sons who were given the task of creating people, the earth and other gods. They began the cyclical pattern of creation and destruction that formed the religious frame to Aztec lives.

The birth of the Sun was a critical occasion because it provided the logic that supported the Aztec practice of human sacrifice: two gods jumped into a fire to create the Sun. The first sun that appeared (our Moon) worried the gods because it might be too bright, so they threw a rabbit at it to dim it (a shape that can sometimes be seen on its surface today). But it did not move. The second sun could only be made to move by more sacrifice, so the remaining gods removed their hearts and sacrificed themselves to make the Sun move across the sky.

And thus, just as the gods sacrificed themselves for the Sun, so the Aztecs believed that people also had to provide blood and hearts to keep the Sun going.

Some of this blood the Aztecs provided by personal bloodletting as part of worship (generally body piercing by thorns through ears, tongues and genitals), but most was by human sacrifice. Those sacrificed were nearly always prisoners captured in battle, which explains why there was such a constant need for wars. This, in turn, accelerated the expansion of the Aztec Empire and explains why people eventually turned so violently against the Aztecs when they were given the chance to side with the invading Spaniards.

Sacrificial knives

The sacrificial knives were made of **obsidian**. Obsidian is a black volcanic glass occurring naturally in Central America. It is rather brittle and when split produces extremely sharp edges – sharper than any known tool, ancient or modern. A well-knapped edge can be sharper than a surgeon's scalpel.

Time

The Aztecs believed that time was divided into a number of ages of existence (we are currently in the fifth age, which is due to end in 2027), each presided over by a different sun, controlled by a different god, and peopled by a different race. Each age was believed to end in a violent catastrophe.

In their own words

Four men stretched the captive out on the sacrificial stone grasping his arms and legs. In the hand of the fire priest lay the knife. When he had split open his breast, he at once seized the heart. And he whose breast he laid open was quite alive... The bodies were rolled down the steps of the temple, and the steps were bathed in blood.

From an account told
to Friar Sahagun

Why you need to know these facts

Unless we understand the logic behind the bloody religious practices of the Aztecs we may fall into the error of thinking that what they did was simply due to bloodlust or, worse, that they were just stupid.

One cannot understand the Aztecs without understanding their religion. They were no less intelligent than us, but as to whether they were as 'civilised' will depend upon your definition of the word.

Vocabulary

Obsidian – very hard stone (black volcanic glass) used by the Aztecs for cutting and weaponry.

Amazing facts

● The hearts of prisoners were removed whilst they were still alive. Their heads were cut off for mounting on skull racks that were next to the pyramid.

● A Spanish witness calculated that the skull rack by the Great Temple could hold over 1 million heads.

Common misconceptions

The Aztecs thought that the Spanish invaders might be gods.

This is most unlikely. Although it was believed that Moctezuma (the Aztec emperor at the time of the Spanish arrival) 'trembled on his throne in the mountains' at the thought of meeting the supernatural Cortés, modern research suggests that this was a rewriting of the events by Aztec historians seeking to explain the sudden end of the Aztec Empire.

Teaching ideas

● When teaching the Aztecs, choose a few questions to answer. You cannot teach everything, so be selective. Make sure you take the opportunity to discuss the Spanish-Aztec culture clash. Although the Spanish admired Aztec achievements, they regarded them as heathens and had no sympathy with their religious practices. However, they did not indulge in ethnic cleansing as is sometimes assumed.

● Imagine that you are an Aztec commoner. Explain to a foreign visitor why so many people have to be killed on the steps of the temple.

Tenochtitlan and Aztec cities

Subject facts

There was no place in the world like the Aztec capital Tenochtitlan; it was unique in size and design. It was a working city built to impress both people and gods and to intimidate enemies. When the Spanish first caught sight of it they were amazed. This was partly because of its size: it was the largest city ever built in the ancient New World and, with nearly a quarter of a million inhabitants, it was larger than any European city at the time.

As the Spanish approached the city along the long, straight causeways, crossing the drawbridges constantly being raised and lowered to let through the trading canoes and flat-bottomed barges, one can imagine their astonishment. Alongside them, as they entered, ran large aqueducts bringing fresh water to the inhabitants.

The city of Tenochtitlan was carefully laid out in a regular grid pattern, with four major avenues which divided it into segments originating from the sacred precinct (see 'City centre' below). The most important axis was east to west – the route of the Sun – and the canals and roads ran at right angles in order that everything followed the same orientation. Small flat-roofed houses clustered together in places, although farmers still coexisted in the city on more spacious plots of firm land. Along the canals and roads the traders plied their wares; most of the heavier loads were transported by water.

In the other city states in central Mexico, the majority of the housing was well spaced out and interspersed with gardens and fields. Houses were not laid out in a formal plan and generally were simple structures built of adobe bricks (unfired bricks that were dried in the sun).

City centre
At the heart of Aztec cities was an open public square bordered by religious and administrative buildings. Tenochtitlan was again

unique, for at its heart was a sacred central walled precinct to which public access was limited. It was square, about 500 metres (1640 feet) across, and packed with temples, altars, shrines, schools and assembly halls. But all this was dominated by the towering twin stairway of the pyramid-temple.

Chinampas

Surrounding Tenochtitlan were fertile fields called **chinampas**, created in the swampy lake areas. Long straight ditches drained away the excess water to form artificial islands, edged with trees to hold the soil in place. Farmers would have been seen canoeing from field to field.

Town and country

When the Spanish first came to Mexico, it was a fairly stable, safe place for the Aztecs, because they dominated the surrounding peoples. The countryside was safe enough to live and work in, so cities were largely places for merchant and workshop activity, not walled defensive retreats as was often the case in Europe. They were quite rural in appearance and there was no sharp division between countryside and town.

Few cities had a population of more than 20,000; the average administrative capital in the Valley of Mexico had around 9000 inhabitants. The smallest cities deserving of the name had around 800 residents but had considerable space given over to farming. Peasants, who were relatively prosperous and not like medieval serfs in Europe, came to the cities daily to attend the markets, to pay taxes and to take part in religious and other festivals.

An open square was at the heart of the city, with the king's palace, a temple and other civic structures arranged on the four sides. The temple was always sited on the east side. A stairway led up the west front of the temple-pyramid to a platform and the roofed temple rooms that always crowned the structure. In the city square there was often a court for playing the game of **tlachtli**.

Tlachtli

We do not have an equivalent of the Aztec ballgame *tlachtli*, because it involved religion, ritual, entertainment, gambling and athleticism. It was kind of tennis played with a hard rubber ball on a court in the shape of a capital 'I'. Without rackets, players (individuals and teams) attempted to put the ball through carved stone rings placed vertically on the central walls. They could only use their hips or knees, and they wore protective clothes made of deerskin. A goal finished the game, but these were apparently rare and points usually decided the issue. These were awarded for particular manoeuvres or skills. The game could last a long time and the winner might be awarded prizes of feathers or even the clothes of the spectators. Games were sacred events that the priests used as omens for the future. Feathers and jade were gambled on the outcome but it was not unknown for farms, children and even personal freedom to be staked.

In their own words

On seeing the ball come at them, as it was about to touch the floor, the players were so quick to turn their knees or buttocks to the ball they returned it with extraordinary swiftness. With this bouncing back and forth they suffered terrible injuries on their knees and thighs.

Diego Durán, a Spanish priest writing about the game

The marketplace

Every city had its market, but the largest in the ancient world was the one in Tlatelolco, which was Tenochtitlan's twin city, and part of the large conurbation now covered by Mexico City. The marketplace was well organised, and policed by up to a dozen judges who held court in a fine building on the edge of the market square. Cheats and thieves could be executed; officials patrolled the stalls checking on the sales. Each type of merchandise had its own particular place in the market and everything was sold by number and measure, but not by weight. Slaves, medicines and dogs for eating could be purchased. You could also have your hair cut or buy a fish pie. Most city markets took place once a week but the largest of all opened every day. Amongst goods spotted by a Spanish observer were stone knives, brass axes, rabbits, honey, sandals, rope, lions, otters, jackals, deer, cotton, henequen (a plant grown for its leaf fibres), salt, beans, herbs, fruit, tripe, maize and cochineal.

The jewel in the crown of Aztec civilisation was its city states, and to understand the Aztecs you must understand this achievement. To understand the significance of Tenochtitlan, for example, you need to grasp the fact that it would have ranked as one of the wonders of the world at that time, and that it exceeded every city in Europe in both size and sophistication.

In their own words

Proud of itself is the city of Mexico-Tenochtitlan.
Here no one fears to die in war.
This is our glory.
This is your command, oh Giver of Life!
Have this in mind, oh princes do not forget it.
Who could conquer Tenochtitlan?
Who could shake the foundation of heaven?

Aztec poem

Why you need to know these facts

Aztec cities overwhelmed the Spanish with their beauty and grandeur when they first came upon them. You cannot understand the Aztec achievement without understanding their cities.

Vocabulary

Chinampa – the Aztec name for a raised field created in a swampy area for agriculture.
Pochteca – professional merchants in the Aztec markets.
Tlachtli – an Aztec ballgame.

Amazing facts

● There were no wheeled vehicles or beasts of burden in ancient Mexico; everything was transported by boat or carried by porters.

- There were no weighing scales in an Aztec market. Goods were sold only by number.
- 'Tenochtitlan' means 'among the stone-cactus fruit'.

Teaching ideas

- Build a model of the heart of the Aztec capital. Make sure that it is correctly orientated. Research the project properly before you begin.
- Create a game like *tlachtli*. Mark out a court and make up the kinds of rules that the Aztecs must have had. Don't be frightened of changing rules to make the game more fun.
- Collect and display (correctly labelled) goods (pictures will do) that could be bought in an Aztec market.
- Act out a scene in the market court where a trader is accused of giving short measure.

War and warriors

Subject facts

Military skills were highly prized by the Aztecs. A council of four noblemen ran the army. Warriors who had earned their position by skill and courage formed the officers corps. To enter the highest order of officers you had to have performed at least 20 deeds of bravery and captured many prisoners. Special headdresses, jewellery and clothing marked out each rank, such as eagle and jaguar warriors.

Ordinary soldiers

The common soldier wore war suits of animal skins, while the nobles had suits woven from feathers that were highly prized. The great mass of infantry wore body paint for identification and fought barefoot. They were armed with stabbing javelins, obsidian-bladed clubs and round, leather-trimmed shields. There was no standing army and men were called up for specific campaigns, the smallest units being led by their own community leaders.

The reason for wars

The main object of battle was to capture prisoners, so the Aztecs had no concept of fighting to the finish. Had they done so, the Spanish would not have escaped from Tenochtitlan after the death of Moctezuma. Battle was an extension of religious practice; indeed, warriors ritually ate flesh taken from the thighs of sacrificed captives. The conquistadores found this beyond their understanding and this kind of cultural incomprehension contributed to the final and fatal conflict with the Aztecs.

Why you need to know these facts

Aztec society was built on military strength. Military skill was needed to subjugate the surrounding tribes and to sustain their religion. Military failure was the occasion of the fall of the Empire.

Amazing facts

Moctezuma sent emissaries to greet Cortés carrying many presents. The Spaniards rejected what the Aztecs regarded as the most significant of their gifts – food (tortillas, turkeys, eggs, guavas and so on) sprinkled with the blood of sacrificed humans.

Teaching ideas

● Make an inventory of Aztec weapons with illustrations and descriptions.
● The main aim of Aztec warfare was to take prisoners, not to kill. Debate how this might have helped the Spanish to defeat the Aztecs even though they were greatly outnumbered.

Resources

In spite of being less easy to resource than British history topics, the Aztecs are nevertheless popular with primary teachers.

One way into this topic, and the source of some interesting resources, are high street shops and supermarkets. Look in food shops for Mexican foods (tortillas, guacamole, etc) that will link to the Aztecs. Because Mexico is a relatively common holiday destination, colourful travel catalogues can be obtained from travel agents. It is possible that you may have a child in your class who has been to Mexico and can recount relevant experiences. Providers of Mexican arts and crafts can also be useful sources, so you might research specialist shops, for example, Quetzal Mexican Arts and Crafts.

Aztec collections in museums can be found but the British Museum in London is, again, an important source: **www.british museum.org**. Some American museums have useful websites and you could make a start with: **www.getty.edu/art/exhibitions/ aztec**. The Pitt Rivers Museum in Oxford is interesting and does cater for primary school visits: **www.prm.ox.ac.uk/primary.html**. Cadbury World in Bourneville, Birmingham is a surprising venue, but there is an interesting display about cocoa that has fascinating and worthwhile material on the Aztecs: **www.cadburyworld.co.uk**.

Books
- *Eyewitness: Aztec* by E. Baquedano (Dorling Kindersley, 2011) – clear, bright and useful; packed with information.
- *Aztec Times* by Antony Mason (Marshall Publishing, 1997) – a comprehensive examination of the topic.
- *Crafts from the Past: The Aztecs* by Gillian Chapman (Harper Collins, 2000) – emphasis here is mainly on crafts rather than the past.
- *Sun Gods and Sacrifice* by P. Steele and F. MacDonald (Southwater, 2004) – as with a number of books on this topic its scope goes beyond the Aztecs to include other Central American civilizations.
- *Aztecs and Incas* by S. Nicholson (Kingfisher, 2000) – a colourful guide to the subject, again going beyond the Aztecs.
- *The Aztec* by A. Santella (Children's Press, 2003).

- *Growing up in Aztec Times* by M. Wood (Troll Communications, 1998).
- *Mexican Pictorial Manuscripts* (The Bodleian Library, Oxford, 1972).

Want to know more?
- *The Aztecs: A Very Short Introduction* by David Carrasco (Oxford University Press, 2012).
- *Aztecs and Maya* by N. James (The History Press, 2009).
- *Mexico* by M. D. Coe and R. Koontz (Thames and Hudson, 2008) – well-illustrated, wide-ranging book containing lots of detail; now in its sixth published edition.
- *The Aztecs* by Richard F. Townsend (Thames and Hudson, 2010) – this revised edition is a pretty comprehensive look at the Aztec empire, warts and all.

The Tudors

The Tudor period was a time of powerful rulers, memorable heroes and heroines, and of a growing awareness of the wider world. England was generally more wealthy, more powerful and more peaceful than ever before. It was also an age of sea exploration, when new trade routes were established and new lands were discovered.

We remember the Tudors for their great literature: for the resonant phrases of Shakespeare and *The Book of Common Prayer*, and for the works of Marlowe and Spencer. We remember, too, religious turmoil when the Church of England was separated from Rome, the monasteries were dissolved, and Catholics and Protestants were both cruelly persecuted in their turn.

Introducing the Tudors

Subject facts

Who were the Tudors?

The Tudor period (1485–1603) and dynasty began when Henry Tudor defeated Richard III at the battle of Bosworth. The year 1485 marked the end of the Wars of the Roses and the beginning of a dynasty that was to last until the death of Elizabeth I in 1603. Henry's grandfather was Welsh and it was his name, *Tewdwr*, that was subsequently treated as a surname by the English.

In Tudor times there was no United Kingdom. Although England and Wales were joined by an Act of Union in 1536, Scotland was a separate kingdom against which the English fought. At the battle of Flodden in 1513, Scotland lost its king, James IV, and the cream of its nobility. In Ireland, attempts to Anglicise the Gaelic Irish largely failed but, in spite of this, Henry VIII called himself 'King of Ireland'.

For most of the Tudor period, the English not only ruled England, but part of France as well. (Until the 1430s England had suzerainty over Bordeaux, a large area of land to the south of it and most of the area to the north of the Loire.) But by 1453, the English had been expelled from everywhere except Calais.

Timeline	
AD 1485	*Battle of Bosworth – Henry Tudor defeats Richard III and becomes Henry VII.*
1492	*Christopher Columbus discovers America.*
1509	*Henry VIII becomes king.*
1511	*Launch of the Mary Rose.*
1513	*Battle of Flodden between England and Scotland. James IV of Scotland killed.*
1519	*Magellan began first* **circumnavigation** *of the world.*
1520	*Field of Cloth of Gold (a meeting between Henry VIII and Francis I of France where a great deal of wealth was on display).*
1534	**Dissolution of the monasteries**.
1536	*England and Wales joined by the Act of Union.*
1539	*Great Bible published in English.*
1545	*Sinking of the Mary Rose.*
1547	*Edward VI becomes king.*
1553	*Mary I becomes queen.*
1558	*Elizabeth I becomes queen.*
1564	*William Shakespeare is born in Stratford-upon-Avon.*
1565	*Hawkins introduced sweet potatoes and tobacco to England.*
1576	*The Theatre opens in Shoreditch.*
1577–80	*Sir Francis Drake's voyage around the world.*
1587	*Drake attacks Cadiz – 'singes the King of Spain's beard'.*
1588	*Defeat of the Spanish Armada.*
1603	*Elizabeth I dies; crown passes to James VI of Scotland.*

How do we know about the Tudors?

English is the key to evidence about the Tudors. It was in this period that official documents gradually moved from being written in Latin to English, so we not only have ready access to colloquial sources in English, but to official ones, too. Although even in English Tudor documents can be hard to read, it does mean that children can begin to tackle original documents for the first time. The Tudor age is also the first period in British history from which common domestic architecture begins to survive, although only houses of the better sort are still standing from the 16th century.

Why you need to know these facts

The Tudor dynasty lasted for just over a century, and during that time England grew economically, militarily and culturally. It managed to keep its independence from its more powerful European neighbours, France and Spain; the foundations of today's predominantly Protestant England were laid and, with the Act of Union, so were the foundations of the present United Kingdom.

Vocabulary

Circumnavigation – to journey around (usually to sail around the world).
Dissolution of the monasteries – the deliberate breaking up of the monasteries and the seizing of their wealth by Henry VIII.

Elizabethan society

Subject facts

Town and country
Daily life was country life for everybody, unless you happened to live in London, which was the only really urban area.

Even Londoners were not far from the countryside. England was relatively undeveloped, a green agricultural land with many deep forests and a population of around 2 million at the start of the period. A century later, the population of England had almost doubled, but the country still produced enough food to support its people. As the land-owning classes became richer, the poor tended to become poorer. Displaced rural peasants wandered the country as vagabonds.

Sickness and health

Life expectancy was about 38 years; plagues and periodic epidemics affected the size of population, especially in towns, and poor sewage disposal aggravated the problem. On the whole, doctors were not much use to the sick, with the practice of bleeding exacerbating rather than aiding recovery. In any case, most people did not have access to doctors but used local traditional treatments. There was no protection against big killers, such as diphtheria or measles, and even a simple fracture could lead to amputation, gangrene and death.

Dress

There was no single Tudor style, and fashions changed just as they do today, although fashion was really only something that concerned the rich – the poor could not afford to be fussy about what they wore. One significant feature of much of the Tudor period, especially during the reign of Henry VIII, was that men were just as brightly dressed as women, if not more so. Men wore hose, similar to modern tights, and a frequently used technique was to slash the sleeves and bodice of the top jacket in order to reveal brightly coloured shirts beneath.

Education

Queen Elizabeth I was well educated, but she was a daughter of the aristocracy. Education was not generally thought to be necessary for girls. People who could afford it (like Shakespeare's parents) sent their sons to school. At least 135 free grammar schools were started during the reign of Elizabeth, although they charged most pupils. Latin, logic and religion were the staple diet of subjects, and the children were force-fed their lessons, if necessary by the use of harsh discipline.

Houses

The houses of the poor have vanished. They were poorly constructed hovels and have not stood the test of time. People lived in simple, usually thatched, cottages on an earthen floor. Most of their daily needs were provided locally and they were never far from a source of water. Life continued largely as it had done for centuries, with an annual timetable dictated by the seasons, the weather, and Holy Days.

The parish church was often the centre of village life and the parson (the *person*) might well be the only man who could read and write in the community. The church bell summoned people to church, attendance at which was compulsory, and it was also used to warn of danger (for example, bells were rung when the Armada approached).

What we commonly regard as Tudor houses, especially the black-and-white half-timbered variety, were largely the substantial dwellings of wealthy yeoman farmers. Many of these have survived. There was a great increase in this type of housebuilding as agriculture flourished in the 1560s–70s.

Large mansions now ceased to be fortified (the country experienced almost unbroken internal peace during the reign of the Tudor monarchs) and were more comfortable than previously. Glass-producing techniques improved and more and more glass windows began to appear. A feature of large houses was often a long gallery, which was used for games, dancing, fencing and simply walking. More fireplaces were constructed and extravagant Tudor chimneys became an ostentatious outward show of an owner's wealth. Hardwick Hall, Compton Wynyates and Hampton Court are fine examples of great Tudor mansions.

Why you need to know these facts

To understand the lives of men and women in Tudor times, we must look beyond political events and the stories of great men and women to see how everyday people coped with everyday priorities.

Common misconceptions

Tudor houses were all black-and-white half-timbered.
Houses were built of local materials because of the difficulty of
transporting heavy materials over long distances. Some were
built entirely of stone, and even brick buildings began to be
more common. Half-timbered houses were most common in
the south and east and places like Cheshire and Herefordshire.
The black-and-white painted appearance is largely a
modern affectation.

Teaching ideas

● Design and build a model of the timber framework of a Tudor
house. You might use centimetre-squared cross-section dowels as
the main model-building material.
● Weave wattle. (I don't advise making daub: cow dung.
Even if it is readily available in your classroom, it might get
up an inspector's nose.)
● Map a suitable local area or street (if you have one). Walk
the ground and mark on all Tudor buildings and 'mock' Tudor
references. How can you tell mock from real?
● Write an estate agent's guide to a Tudor house.

Tudor monarchs

Subject facts

Henry VII (1485–1509)

Defeated Richard III at Bosworth and ended the Wars of the
Roses. By strong as well as diplomatic action he brought his
rich and powerful subjects to heel and stopped the medieval
warring that had troubled the country. His wife, Elizabeth of York,
is the figure that has been used on playing cards for the last 500
years – they were invented during his reign.

Henry VIII (1509–1547)

Second son of Henry VII. Although he was talented (he was
the first English king to write, print and publish a book),
his ambitions to rule France, to dominate the Church, and to
produce a son and heir caused much anguish in his reign.
He could not stand being thwarted. When the Church opposed
him over his wish to divorce and remarry, he dispensed with
Cardinal Wolsey (who died en route to his trial) and established
himself as the head of the Church of England. He then dissolved
the monasteries and seized their wealth. Henry built up a strong
navy but ruled without a standing army.

Edward VI (1547–1553)

Son of Henry VIII and his third wife, Jane Seymour, Edward
ruled from the age of nine until his death aged 15. Without a
strong adult ruler, the country began to drift into factionalism.
Nevertheless, the pious Edward accelerated England's move
towards Protestantism. His reign saw the introduction of
the *Book of Common Prayer* (compiled by Thomas Cranmer)
and greater uniformity of worship.

Mary I (1553–1558)

England's first woman ruler, daughter of Henry VIII and his
first wife, Catherine of Aragon, hers was not a happy reign.
Her Catholic fervour and intolerance led to some 300 people
being burned at the stake for their religious beliefs, including
the bishops Latimer, Ridley and Cranmer – hence her nickname
'Bloody Mary'. She married a Catholic (Philip II of Spain) and
subsequently joined Spain in a disastrous war against France.
She lost Calais, which was England's last French possession.

Elizabeth I (1558–1603)

Daughter of Henry VIII and Anne Boleyn. After narrowly
surviving accusations of being a traitor to her sister Mary,
she eventually not only gained the throne upon Mary's
death, but also kept it for 44 years. She returned England
to Protestantism, but in contrast to her sister she was
moderate in actions and beliefs. By skilful political manipulation
she kept a strong hold on the reins of government and kept her

kingdom intact. She kept everyone guessing about whom she would marry and then married no-one. She was educated as well as clever, and was fluent in several languages. She had a keen eye for talent and was served by outstanding advisers.

Why you need to know these facts

The influence of Tudor monarchs upon the shape of the period was enormous, and their characters and actions need to be understood.

Teaching ideas

● Choose a Tudor monarch (different groups could be allocated a monarch each), and write an obituary for him or her. Include a portrait if you can. Use the internet to find more information.
● In groups or as a class, make up a mnemonic or rhyme that will help you to remember the names and order of the Tudor monarchs.
● Write a script for a radio interview of a monarch from the Tudor period. Imagine that you are a radio presenter – what would you like to ask the monarch, and how would they answer? You could act this out for a class assembly.

The wives of Henry VIII

Subject facts

Even by modern Hollywood standards, having six wives is an achievement of some note. Fortunately, the methods by which Henry VIII disposed of one wife before moving on to the next is not something that happens today, and were shocking and callous even then.

Catherine of Aragon

She was the wife of Henry's dead brother Arthur. She gave birth to a daughter, the future Mary I, but in the absence of a male heir Henry divorced her without the Pope's consent, and broke the English Church away from Rome.

Anne Boleyn

Passionate love, while he was still married to Catherine, turned to passionate hate after the birth of Elizabeth (the future queen). Anne was accused of adultery and beheaded.

Jane Seymour

Bore Henry the son he craved, but died 12 days later.

Anne of Cleves

Anne turned out to be less of a beauty than Henry had been led to believe. He married her under protest to secure an alliance with German Protestants and balance the military threat from France and Spain. But when France and Spain, themselves at loggerheads, no longer posed the same degree of threat, the alliance and the marriage lost their purpose. Soon Henry had the marriage **annulled** on grounds of non-consummation and Anne was pensioned off.

In their own words

I liked her before not well, now I like her much worse.

Henry VIII on Anne of Cleves

Catherine Howard

Catherine was much younger than Henry, and was a pawn in the hands of her ambitious uncles. Henry found out about her adultery and she was tried and beheaded.

Catherine Parr

An intelligent woman already twice widowed when Henry married her. Catherine's interest in radical Protestantism was nearly her undoing. When she agreed to yield to her husband in religious matters, investigations of her actions stopped on the king's orders. She nursed and outlived him.

Why you need to know these facts

The treatment of Henry's wives is significant in that it reveals the ruthlessness with which the passionate Henry could act. His actions affected the future of the Church and the succession.

Vocabulary

Annul – to cancel, especially the legality of a marriage.

Amazing facts

For nine days in 1553, England was ruled by a young girl, Lady Jane Grey. She was proclaimed queen by a faction, led by the Duke of Northumberland, in an attempt to prevent the Catholic Mary Tudor from ascending the throne. The coup collapsed because Northumberland was widely detested. Jane Grey was beheaded. She was only 17.

Common misconceptions

Tradition (not evidence) has it that the crown of England was found under a gorse bush after the battle of Bosworth and then placed on Henry Tudor's head.

● Make a chart that will help the children to learn and remember the names of the wives of Henry VIII and what happened to them.
● Learn how to dance a period dance that would have been popular at court. A Spanish pavane is fairly straightforward.

Henry VIII and the break with Rome

Subject facts

Religious pressure for change already existed, and in many parts of Europe a Protestant reformation was taking place. Henry's need for money and a wife who would give him a male heir merely provided the occasion for the split from the Roman Church.

Henry wanted to divorce Catherine of Aragon and marry Anne Boleyn. He ordered his chief adviser in such matters, Cardinal Wolsey, to arrange his divorce by asking the Pope to agree. Wolsey failed and was sacked. Henry then cleared the way for his new wife by ignoring the Pope's view and divorcing Catherine. He cut all legal and financial ties with Rome and made himself head of the Church in England in an Act of Supremacy (1534).

Sir Thomas More (1478–1535) was one of the casualties of Henry's action. More was a scholar and a statesman – a Renaissance humanist. He rose to be Lord Chancellor but opposed the king's divorce and remarriage. When he opposed the Act of Supremacy he was beheaded.

Henry sent his Vicar General, Thomas Cromwell, to organise an audit of monastic life: he had his eyes on the extensive wealth of the monasteries. Many clerics still acknowledged the Pope as their leader and some lived like rich country gentlemen. Although monastic ideals were not always observed, Cromwell's reports were probably biased to satisfy the king's wishes. Henry was given, in Cromwell's reports, the ammunition to dissolve the monasteries and confiscate their wealth, which he did. Many beautiful buildings were destroyed when the monasteries were dissolved in 1534 – church plate was melted down for cash and the nuns and monks turned out onto the streets. It was not an unpopular measure at the time.

After Henry VIII died, the nature of religion in England continued to change. But for the Catholic interlude under Mary Tudor, England became more clearly Protestant in Tudor times. The Mass was renamed Holy Communion, many local Saints' days were abolished, and traditions like Plough Monday and maypoles were stopped. A *Book of Common Prayer* was introduced for the first time in 1549.

Why you need to know these facts

The Church of England resulted from the split with the Roman Catholic Church. This affected the way England has been governed since, the nature of the Church in England, and the subsequent course of this nation's history.

Teaching ideas

● Investigate the difference between Catholic and Protestant. Visit local churches or invite local incumbents to talk to the class.
● Listen to some Tudor music, such as 'Greensleeves'.
● Use the internet to investigate monastic sites in Britain that were destroyed at the dissolution of the monasteries. Prepare brief 'tourist's guides' to some of the destinations, such as Fountains Abbey.

Henry VIII and the Mary Rose

Subject facts

In 1545 Francis I of France sent a fleet to attack England. With 235 ships and 30,000 men, it was larger than the Armada. It sailed round the Isle of Wight to attack Portsmouth and was met by an English fleet of 60 ships led by the *Great Harry* and the *Mary Rose*. Henry watched the battle from Southsea Castle. For reasons that are still not clear, the *Mary Rose* foundered. Water entered through her gunports and she sank so quickly that most of the crew drowned. Only about a dozen of the 700 crew survived. The French boasted that they had sunk the ship, but bad seamanship seems to be the most likely cause. The French troops that made it ashore made no progress and returned to France.

Why you need to know these facts

Tudor sea power began with Henry VIII, and he laid the foundations for English maritime exploits in the reign of Elizabeth I. He created an effective navy, which could compete with the maritime supremacy of Spain. Portsmouth dockyard was built, 80 ships were added to the navy and the navy and army were separated for the first time.

Amazing facts

In 1982 the *Mary Rose* was raised from the sea bed. It provided an enormous amount of evidence about the crew and life on board a Tudor ship. Among the finds were 168 yew bows and 3000 arrows (each 79cm long), games, musical instruments, a surgeon's chest, tableware, sewing kits and clothes.

Teaching ideas

Investigate the mystery of the sinking of the *Mary Rose*. Is it a case of whodunnit? or whatdunnit?

Elizabeth I

Subject facts

Elizabeth I remains one of the most remarkable British monarchs, and one of the most important in the Tudor dynasty. Elizabeth's skill at maintaining the integrity of her kingdom is legendary and she needed all her considerable intelligence to survive in the climate of intrigue that was the Tudor court.

Mary Queen of Scots

One of Elizabeth's first problems was to deal with the threats to her throne that came from her cousin, Mary Stuart – Mary Queen of Scots. Mary, whose mother was French, spent 13 years in France. She was married briefly to the young French king, but he died after two years, and she was forced to return to Scotland. As a devout Catholic she did not last long when faced with a Protestant hierarchy there, especially the extremist Protestant reformer and misogynist John Knox. He wrote a book *The First Blast of the Trumpet Against the Monstrous Regiment of Women*.

But Mary was an attractive woman and at first gained popularity with the people of Edinburgh. She married her cousin, the lusty womaniser Lord Darnley, thus strengthening her claim to the English throne (he was the grandson of Henry VIII's sister) but weakening her public and political image. Mary soon felt lonely and was neglected by her husband, so she turned to David Rizzio, her private secretary, for advice. Darnley became jealous and, one night, Rizzio was seized in the queen's presence and murdered on the stairs in Holyrood Palace. Darnley was there and Mary was forced to flee.

Intrigues continued: Mary fell in love with the Earl of Bothwell, then Darnley was mysteriously murdered. Bothwell was found not guilty of the crime after a farcical trial – but it was an intrigue too far. Mary married Bothwell and the Scots turned against her. She rapidly abdicated in favour of her infant son James and fled on horseback to England for safety.

Unfortunately, there she became the focus of Catholic plots. She was imprisoned and continued to plot against Elizabeth, who eventually, and reluctantly, had her executed for treason in 1587.

The marriage problem and Essex

The other problem which dogged Elizabeth was the constant attempt to marry her off. Marriage was, for a monarch, a matter of major political significance. First there was the need to secure the succession; then there was the matter of forging a political alliance through marriage (a very delicate matter); and thirdly there was always the question of a bad match handing power to an ambitious, unscrupulous or unsuitable man. Elizabeth solved the problem by keeping everyone guessing and ultimately not marrying at all.

There was, however, no shortage of suitors. Robert Devereux, the second Earl of Essex, was one suspected lover. A clever, literate man, he soon became a favourite of Elizabeth, but fell out of favour when his clandestine marriage was discovered. Nevertheless he rose to be a privy councillor and take the title Earl Marshall. He was strong-willed and hard to control. He had a great quarrel with Elizabeth when he turned his back on her, and she boxed his ears. The quarrel was never properly made up and, after serving in Ireland, he eventually ended up in prison. He formed a mad plot to remove Elizabeth's councillors and tried to start a rebellion in London. As a consequence he was beheaded in 1601.

Why you need to know these facts

The behaviour of the ruling classes, Tudor court intrigues, and the love affairs of Tudor monarchs were of great significance in this period. The marriages of monarchs were not personal events, but political ones that could resolve conflicts or even cause wars.

Vocabulary

Progresses – Elizabeth I journeyed around her kingdom every summer in order to be seen by as many people as possible. These were known as 'progresses'.

Amazing facts

On one of her summer **progresses**, Queen Elizabeth stayed
with Lord North for three days. Together with her entourage
she consumed 1200 chickens, 67 sheep, 34 pigs, 33 geese and
2500 eggs.

Teaching ideas

Examine Tudor costume through pictures. Make a collage
reproduction of a famous portrait. Try to match the colours
and stick to natural fabrics.

Tudor seafarers and explorers

Subject facts

John and Sebastian Cabot

John Cabot (1425–1500) and his son Sebastian (1474–1557)
lived in Venice before making Bristol their home in about 1490.
Enjoying the patronage of Henry VII, John sailed with his three
sons from Bristol in 1497 in two ships. They looked for a north-
west passage to the riches of the east; instead they found land
not seen by Europeans since Viking times – Nova Scotia and
Cape Breton Island. Sebastian was a cartographer and worked
for both the Spanish and Henry VIII. He was made inspector of
the Navy by Edward VI and in 1499 claimed credit for exploring
the north-west passage, credit that should have been his father's.

John Hawkins (1532–1595)

John Hawkins was one of those swashbuckling adventurers who
cut their teeth harrying Spanish treasure ships in the West Indies.
But he was later appointed treasurer of Elizabeth's navy and
helped to make it into the formidable force that was to defeat

the Spanish Armada. His other major claim to fame is that he was one of the first Englishmen to run the trading route that led from Africa to Central America, carrying slaves. This brought him into direct conflict with the Spanish, which encouraged him into further piratical activity.

Francis Drake (c.1540–1596)

Drake was one of the most successful privateers and a constant thorn in the side of the Spanish. In 1572, for example, with two ships and 73 men, he attacked a Spanish fleet near Nombre de Dios and captured so much treasure that he could not carry it all away. To the Spanish he was a pirate; to the English a hero at a time when England was contesting supremacy of the seas with the Spanish.

Under the sponsorship of Elizabeth I, Drake became the first Englishman to circumnavigate the globe (1577–80). With five ships he set out to explore the Strait of Magellan, returning to England via the Cape of Good Hope. Only one ship, the *Golden Hind*, made it back to England and his search for a north-west passage also failed. But he sailed around Cape Horn, attacked Spanish ships on the Peruvian coast, and renamed California 'New Albion'. He crossed the Pacific Ocean and traded for spices in the Far East before returning to Plymouth.

Drake was involved in other state-sponsored adventures, mainly aimed at acquiring treasure and weakening the fleets of Spain and Portugal. In 1587, Drake destroyed between two and three dozen Spanish ships in Cadiz where they were preparing for an invasion of England. This delayed the Armada for a year.

The Spanish Armada, 1588

Drake (*Revenge*), Hawkins (*Victory*), Howard (*Ark Royal*) and Frobisher (*Triumph*) were part of a talented and experienced roll call of captains whose expertise and bravery helped to defeat the Spanish attempt to invade England in 1588. Spain was tired of the English interference with her treasure ships sailing from the New World and recognized that England was challenging Spanish supremacy at sea. But the hostility between the two countries ran deeper: Spain was Catholic, England was Protestant, and Philip of Spain had been Queen Mary's husband. For him it was a religious campaign to put a Catholic monarch back on the English throne. Elizabeth had been declared a usurper and a heretic and excommunicated by the Pope in 1570, so the Pope gave his blessing to Philip's crusade.

It was an ambitious move on the part of Philip of Spain. The Armada was commanded by the Duke Medina Sidonia (who was not a sailor and ill-suited to his command) and consisted of 130 ships manned by 8000 seamen. Also on board was the Army of Flanders (about 20,000 soldiers). Sidonia had orders to sail across the Channel and land near Margate before thrusting northwards towards London.

The Armada sailed up the Channel but the English fleet, under the command of Lord Howard of Effingham, harassed them. The English fleet was forced by the direction of the wind to wait until they were behind the Armada before setting sail, so they appeared to the west of the Spanish and snapped at their heels without inflicting much harm. Both sides expressed admiration for the seamanship of the other: the Spanish holding firm to a difficult crescent formation up the Channel, the English nipping around their flanks carefully avoiding getting surrounded by the larger Spanish vessels. Many suitable landing places were passed, because Medina Sidonia kept to his orders to go for the Margate area. The English, not knowing this, feared a landing on the Isle of Wight and continued to harass until the fleet anchored off Calais. Both fleets were by now running low on ammunition.

English fire ships were sent in at night, which caused the Spanish to panic and slip their moorings. Although the Spanish intended to return at daybreak, tides swept the Armada northwards. Spanish ships, now out of formation, became isolated and were attacked, and bad weather finally forced them to head for home round the north of Scotland. Many of the ships were wrecked; only 53 returned to Spain.

In spite of this disaster, other Armadas were planned, and in 1595 the Spanish attacked again, this time destroying Penzance, but other attempts were driven back by storms. In the early Stuart period (1604), peace was signed between England and Spain and there were no more Armadas.

Walter Ralegh and exploration

Walter (later Sir Walter) Ralegh is a Tudor figure worthy of study because he is representative of the explorers and seafarers that were responsible for extending knowledge of the New World and for increasing England's wealth and influence in Europe.

He was almost the model hero: six feet tall with thick black hair, educated (at Oxford), adventurous and brave. He could also be headstrong and was once thrown into prison for causing an affray in Westminster. Such a striking character was, perhaps, bound to be noticed at court, where he rapidly became one of Queen Elizabeth's favourites. One story of how Ralegh came to the Queen's attention describes how Elizabeth was about to step out of her coach into a pool of water when the young Ralegh stepped forward and placed his cloak over the puddle. There is no historical proof that this actually happened, although the action would have been consistent with his gallant character.

Ralegh was responsible for making smoking fashionable at court, but he was not responsible for bringing tobacco back to England in the first place – Ralegh received his tobacco from Drake.

'Piratical' is a good word to describe Ralegh's early career as an explorer. He sailed from the coast of Devon seeking not new lands but Spanish treasure ships to plunder. After rising to an important position at court, he was made Vice-Admiral of the Western Counties and given the title Sir Walter Ralegh. He spent a great deal of his own money trying to build a **colony** in Virginia but without much success, although he brought back the potato plant. Potatoes were first planted at one of Ralegh's homes in Ireland.

It is as a seafarer that Ralegh lays most of his claim to fame. He fought against the Spanish at Cadiz (and was wounded), he searched for gold in South America, and captured and plundered Spanish treasure ships. He had another spell in prison for angering the queen by having an affair with one of her maids, and finally, when the queen died, his enemies conspired to get him confined to the Bloody Tower as a traitor. He spent years as a prisoner carrying out experiments, making medicines and writing a history of the world. Queen Elizabeth had been his main protector, but when he failed to find gold in South America after being released from prison, he was doomed. Partly to appease the Spanish, who desired to see the end of Ralegh, he was beheaded in 1618, aged 66.

Why you need to know these facts

This was the time when Europeans explored huge areas of the world, in effect for the first time. The Tudors may have been searching for routes to the spices of the Orient or for new land or gold, but in doing so they colonized continents, opened trade routes, and introduced new foods and goods to Europe. Their legacy shaped today's world.

Vocabulary

Colony – a group of people who have made new homes in a foreign country.
Empire – a collection of countries and peoples ruled by one person or state.
Scurvy – a disease caused by the lack of Vitamin C, which results in bleeding under the skin, anaemia, and spongy gums. Suffered by sailors on long journeys without fruit or vegetables.

Amazing facts

● Many of the risky journeys of exploration by sea were made seeking a route to the east and valuable spices. Today spices are commonplace, but in Tudor times men risked everything to trade in cargoes such as nutmeg, cinnamon, cloves, mace, pepper and ginger.
● A sailor's diet was so poor that **scurvy** (due to lack of Vitamin C) killed many on long journeys – an estimated 10,000 died during Elizabeth's reign from this cause. Live animals were taken on board for lengthy sea voyages, if possible, and dried fish, rice, ship's biscuits, lentils, cheese, chickpeas and salted meat. Wine was preferred to water, which soon turned green on board and became undrinkable.

Common misconceptions

Drake played bowls while the Armada approached.

The English did have to wait for the Armada to pass to windward before they could sail, and perhaps Drake did play bowls before he sailed. But the only evidence is a comment, made years after the event by a Spanish writer, that 'the English were at bowls upon the Hoe at Plymouth'.

The common spelling of Ralegh is Raleigh.

Ralegh was never spelled Raleigh in his lifetime, although today you will see both spellings. Modern historians, as opposed to school textbook writers, favour Ralegh, as that was the way he himself spelled his name.

Teaching ideas

● Investigate which foods were brought to the Tudor table from newly discovered lands.
● Find out about life on board a Tudor ship. How did the sailors tell the time? What kinds of food did they eat? How did they navigate?
● On an outline map of the world, mark the places that were visited by famous Tudor sailors. You may be able to plot some of their voyages.
● Have a celebration of an old Tudor tradition such as maypole dancing.

Elizabethan theatre

Subject facts

Actors and the theatre were, for a long time, regarded as wicked. Puritans once banned plays, and women were not allowed on the stage. Instead, boys played female parts. But in later Tudor times, the world of the travelling player, scraping a living on the edge of legality by performing in the open air or inn yards, changed forever. Queen Elizabeth enjoyed plays, so performing and writing them gradually became more respectable. In 1577, James Burbage at Shoreditch erected the first purpose-built playhouse, called The Theatre. His son Richard built The Globe in 1599.

William Shakespeare (1564–1616)

Shakespeare was born on St George's day (23 April) in the same year as Christopher Marlowe, the other leading playwright of the era. Shakespeare was the son of a glover from Stratford-upon-Avon, and his mother, Mary Arden, was a farmer's daughter. He was given a decent education in Stratford and, having married Anne Hathaway, another farmer's daughter, he made his home in London. In the early 1590s he was performing on the stage with Richard Burbage. He formed a relationship with the Burbages and wrote many plays for them. Gradually he began to acquire fame and fortune and purchased a house and land in Stratford in preparation for retirement. He had three children, Susanna and twins Hamnet and Judith.

As well as many plays, he wrote over 150 sonnets and a number of narrative poems. Shakespeare had an unequalled genius that flowered at a time when the performance of plays was becoming respectable.

Why you need to know these facts

The theatre as we know it began in the late 16th century. This is the era of Shakespeare, arguably the greatest poet and playwright the world has ever known.

Amazing facts

The stealing of plots was rife in Shakespeare's time and still goes on. The musical *West Side Story* is a reworking of Shakespeare's *Romeo and Juliet*.

Teaching ideas

Write a newspaper report of a visit to the Tudor theatre. Remember the cutpurses as well as the play.

Resources

You will not have to look far for places to visit in England and you are likely to have a worthwhile museum or historic Tudor site in your county. Most of the places worth visiting are also worth contacting for resources and teachers' packs. For Tudor houses see the National Trust (**www.nationaltrust.org.uk**) and English Heritage (**www.english-heritage.org.uk**) but there are also specialised museums to consider. There are so many places and museum collections that you will be spoilt for choice. Here are a few you can start with:

- **www.wealddown.co.uk** – open-air museum with more than 50 historic buildings.
- **www.avoncroft.org.uk** – museum of historic buildings.
- **www.shakespearesglobe.com** – a reconstruction of the Globe Theatre.
- **www.maryrose.org** – museum of the infamous ship.
- **www.shakespeare.org.uk** – Shakespeare Birthplace Trust.

Books

The Tudors are a very popular subject with adults – just think of the number of TV programmes and films there have been on the period – so you will have little difficulty finding books, of all kinds, on the period. More recently published books listed below are still in print, but those not in print are widely available, not only from County Library collections but also from many booksellers. Books for children can also be good for teachers seeking readily accessible data and pictures. The first three titles listed are specifically for teachers:

● *Tudor Times* by Jo Lawrie and Paul Noble (Collins, 1998) –
a resource book with numerous worksheets and teaching ideas.
● *A Teacher's Guide to Using Portraits* by Susan Morris (English
Heritage, 1989) – full of practical advice and teaching strategies.
● *No Fuss: Year 4 Photocopiables* by P. and J. Noble (Scholastic, 2008).
● *On the Trail of the Tudors in Britain* by Richard Wood (Franklin
Watts, 1999) – this books scurries all over Britain to seek out
what the Tudors have left behind them.
● *The Orchard Book of Shakespeare Stories* by Andrew Matthews
and Angela Barrett (Orchard, 2001) – an excellent book with
glorious illustrations.
● *Explorers of the New World* by C. Mooney (Nomad Press, 2011).
● *Eyewitness: Tudor* (Dorling Kindersley, 2011) – can
be appreciated at several levels, although the text is for
upper juniors.
● *Daily Life in a Tudor House* by Laura Wilson (Heinemann, 1995) –
it is worth seeking out a copy of this informative picture book.
● *Look Inside a Tudor Warship* by Brian Moses (Hodder Wayland,
1998) – still widely available in children's libraries.
● *Queen Elizabeth I* by Peggy Burns (Hodder Wayland, 1999).
● *Tudors and Stuarts* by F. Patchett, Kate Davies, Rob Lloyd Jones
and Conrad Mason (Usborne, 2008) – information in an easily
digestible form.

Want to know more?
● *A Brief History of the Tudor Age* by Jasper Ridley (Robinson, 2002).
● *The Tudors* by Richard Rex (Amberley, 2011) – an illustrated
history of the dynasty.
● *The Tudors: A Very Short Introduction* by John Guy (Oxford
University Press, 2000) – a compact book written by a leading
expert in the field.
● *Henry* by David Starkey (Harper Perrenial, 2008) – written to
accompany a Channel 4 programme; both scholarly and readable.
● *The Elizabethans* by A. N. Wilson (Hutchinson, 2011) – a book
of impressive scope.
● *Voyages and Discoveries* by Richard Hakluyt, edited
by J. Beeching (Penguin Books, 1982) – contains Drake's
circumnavigation and the Armada account and is, of course,
an original source.

- *The Tudor Chronicles* by Susan Doran (Quercus, 2008) – a very weighty coffee table book for the enthusiast.
- **www.bbc.co.uk/learningzone/clips/Tudor%20clothes** – BBC audio and video clips about Tudor clothing.
- **www.tudorbritain.org** – an education website about the Tudors, a collaboration between the Victoria and Albert Museum and the National Archives.

The Victorians

During the reign of Queen Victoria, Britain established a vast empire and became the most powerful and wealthy nation in the world. The Victorian legacy remains very conspicuous in Britain today – most hospitals, schools and a large part of the housing stock are Victorian, and people still refer to 'Victorian values'. Although the British Empire has long since disintegrated it is responsible for making Britain the multi-ethnic country that it is today.

Introducing the Victorians

Subject facts

How do we know about the Victorians?

Evidence about the Victorians is overwhelming in quantity. They created much of the urban landscape of Britain, and if we look around it is not long before we see a Victorian house, shop, park or statue. Street names are often Victorian, there may even be a Victorian postbox on a nearby corner.

Documentary evidence of every kind also abounds, but in particular we have regular and systematic government records (the census, for example) kept by law for the first time. We also have official maps (another first) and photographs. The Victorians invented photography and they played with it like a new toy. Photographs bring a new dimension to our knowledge of the past and the Victorian period is the first for which such evidence is available.

Timeline	
1837	Queen Victoria ascends the throne aged 18 years. Fox Talbot invents photography.
1840	Victoria marries Prince Albert. Houses of Parliament and Nelson's Column erected. Transport of criminals to New South Wales ends. Penny Post introduced.
1842	The Mines Act stops children under ten working in the mines. Income tax introduced.
1844	Factory Act limits children's working hours in factories to six-and-a-half hours a day.
1851	Great Exhibition in Hyde Park (Crystal Palace).
1854–56	Crimean War.
1861	Prince Albert dies of typhoid.
1862	The Queen's Silver Jubilee (25 years). First cricket tour of Australia. Education Act sets up Board Schools to provide schools in every area. Alexander Graham Bell invents the telephone.
1880	Education becomes compulsory.
1887	Queen Victoria's Golden Jubilee (50 years). First Sherlock Holmes novel written by Arthur Conan Doyle. First Ediswan (Edison and Swan) electric lightbulb. Baden-Powell founds the Boy Scouts.
1897	Queen Victoria's Diamond Jubilee (60 years).
1900	First underground electric railway opens in London.
1901	Queen Victoria dies aged 81 years.

Victorian society

Subject facts

Rich and poor

Many factory owners in the 19th century became very wealthy and the large houses of these newly rich families can still be seen around Britain's industrial towns today. One of the strange facts about Victorian Britain is that within such a wealthy nation abject poverty could still exist. It worried people at the time: the rich got richer, the nation got richer, hospitals, schools, parks and public buildings were erected on a grand scale, yet the Victorians constantly struggled with the problem of the poor. It was the stuff of parliamentary debate, legislation and literature.

The problem, which threatened to overwhelm the Victorians, was probably the result of their success. The population of Britain grew at an astonishing rate: in 30 years (1871–1901), the population of London grew from 4 million to 6.5 million. Nevertheless, better food, housing and clothing caused the high Victorian mortality rates to start to decline and the lot of the poor generally improved. Birth rates were high and houses were needed quickly so they tended to be built speedily and without proper care. Perhaps the real surprise is that the Victorians coped with the problem as well as they did. During the Victorian period, the quality of housing did gradually improve for the majority of people, but for the poorest 20 per cent it was probably as bad at the beginning of the 20th century as it had been at the beginning of Victoria's reign.

During the latter part of the century there was a growth in the number of charities set up to deal with the problems of poverty, such as the Poor Children's Boot Fund, the Country Holiday Society and the Schools Cheap Dinner Society. There were also state efforts to improve living conditions, indeed the Victorians became very conscious about public health. Local authorities established by the Victorians began to regulate shops and organise street cleaning. Water supplies and sewage disposal became a priority.

Workhouses

From early in the period (1834), workhouses had been set up to cater for the destitute – but these were dire places. In 1840 there was a public outcry when it was discovered that the inmates of Andover Workhouse were so hungry that they were gnawing bones they had been given to crush into fertilizer.

The middle classes

Middle-class houses were large and so were most families. This meant that there was plenty of employment for servants. Butlers, cooks, gardeners and maids were employed to do the menial tasks of the house: cleaning the grates, laying tables, emptying slop buckets and so on. Some servants lived in, and were often accommodated 'below stairs' in fairly cramped conditions.

Running a large home was far more labour intensive than it is today, but in the last decades of the century technological advances began to decrease the drudgery (flushing lavatories, vacuum cleaners, electric ovens and kettles, for example). Although uniforms, board and lodgings were provided for servants, their lives were closely controlled (advertisements required 'no followers', which meant no boyfriends) and wages were very low. An important servant, such as a cook, might earn £25 a year but a scullery maid might earn as little as £9 a year and have little time off for seeing her family.

Holidays and entertainment

Towards the end of the century people had more money and more time to enjoy themselves. Watching and taking part in sport became a national pastime and most well-known British sporting events, like the FA Cup Final, date from this period, as do many national sporting organisations. The Wimbledon tennis championships began in 1874 and the Football Association started to organise the game in 1863. Cycling became incredibly popular: the Cyclists Touring Club was founded in 1878 and there were over 2000 local cycling clubs by 1901.

Travel was relatively easy and cheap. People were able to get out into the countryside under their own steam or by railway. The Victorians virtually invented the idea of 'the seaside', and special railway excursion trains sped them to where they could stroll along the promenade or walk on a pier constructed specially for that purpose. Seaside places close to big industrial centres (such as Blackpool, Bridlington, Skegness and Southend) were extremely popular and could become dominated by workers from particular cities when their factories closed for the local holidays. Thomas Cook started his travel firm in 1841 and made a big profit running excursion trains to the Great Exhibition (see pages 185–6).

Going abroad on a cultural tour became popular with the wealthy – often it was seen as part of the education of a young person. Queen Victoria set an example by favouring holidays abroad, and the wealthy British helped contribute to the creation of the holiday resorts of northern France and the Riviera. For many in the Civil Service and the military, of course, the Empire gave them the opportunity to see the world.

But there was plenty of pleasure to be had at home. Working-class theatres, called 'music halls', were very popular for a night out and audiences flocked to see stars such as Lillie Langtry and Marie Lloyd. Public houses also grew in popularity with the working classes, causing an increase in the problem of alcoholism. Organisations such as the Salvation Army and the temperance movement fought hard to rescue people from such excesses.

Why you need to know these facts

Understanding the past is about understanding people and the way they lived. Even though the Victorian age was a period of astonishing invention and technological change, it is the impact that these advances had on the lives of individuals that is important.

Amazing facts

In the 1860s the average Victorian family had five or six children.

- The children could create a Victorian portrait gallery of leading figures from the period. They could draw information and pictures from the internet or simply create 'pen portraits'. Groups of children could play a game of 'Who's who?', matching descriptions with characters from the portrait gallery.
- Set up a classroom museum of Victorian artefacts and pictures (check the school contents insurance first). Your local museum service may loan out items and children could be encouraged to bring things to school (coins, stamps, samplers, irons, washing dollies and so on).

Queen Victoria and her family

Subject facts

Although Queen Victoria was not a powerful ruler in the old sense, she lived for a long time and left her mark, not only on the period but also on generations after her. She gave her name to an age.

The queen

Victoria became queen as a girl of 18 and reigned for longer than any other British monarch, before or since (63 years). (Elizabeth II, the current monarch, will overtake this milestone in September 2015.) Victoria was born in Kensington Palace in 1819 to the fourth son of George III. She married her cousin, Prince Albert of Saxe-Coburg, in 1840. Prince Albert died at the early age of 42, but she bore him nine children – five boys and four girls. At her Diamond Jubilee in 1897 she had 29 grandchildren.

Most of Victoria's children married into other royal families in Europe. Her eldest son, Edward, married Alexandra, daughter of Christian IX of Denmark and later became Edward VII. Victoria was a lively child with a talent for drawing and painting. She was intelligent and, when she was queen, learned Hindustani so that she could talk with her favourite Indian servants. She also liked to keep a diary, which has revealed many details about her life and attitudes, although her daughter Beatrice destroyed some of this valuable evidence after her mother's death.

Victoria was besotted with Albert and their marriage was a very happy one. After Albert's death in 1861, Victoria went into a prolonged period of mourning from which she never fully recovered. She became known as the 'Widow of Windsor' and refused to be seen in public – even to open Parliament – and this made her very unpopular. But she lived long and her feelings changed. In 1876 she was given the title 'Empress of India'.

Because of her family ties to many of the rulers in Europe, she was also called the 'Grandmother of Europe'. Victoria, the Princess Royal, married Friedrich III the German Emperor, and this provided a strong Anglo-German link that proved embarrassing when World War I started.

In their own words

We are not interested in the possibilities of defeat;
they do not exist.

Queen Victoria visiting troops
after a British 'reversal' in battle

Prince Albert and the Great Exhibition of 1851

Albert was never popular in his lifetime, partly because he was foreign, and also because he attempted to promote liberal and progressive movements in the country. But as the Prince Consort he did have influence, and the Queen doted on him. The Great Exhibition was one of Albert's successes. With his support and the organisational skill of Henry Cole, the Exhibition preparations forged ahead in the face of initial public apathy and some outright opposition. But the idea gained momentum; public subscriptions to fund the project were sought, and the Queen herself donated £1000.

The Exhibition was intended to be about industrial progress, trade and the superiority of British design. The themes were Progress, Work, Religion and Peace. There were over 100,000 exhibits and price labels were strictly forbidden. It was an amazing success – even the public toilets made a profit. People came on day excursions using the new and extensive railway network, some using trains for the first time. On the busiest day 93,224 visitors entered the building.

The building itself was a wonder. The design, by Joseph Paxton, was chosen as the result of a competition that produced 233 entries. The building was originally erected in Hyde Park and was made of cast iron and glass, hence the name 'Crystal Palace'. It took six months to complete. The building did not remain there long and was moved to Sydenham when the Exhibition closed, where it stood until 1936 when it was destroyed by fire. It was over three times the length of St Paul's Cathedral and contained 293,655 panes of glass.

The profit from the Exhibition, some £186,000, was used to purchase the South Kensington sites upon which many of London's leading public buildings were erected (including, for example, the Victoria and Albert Museum and the Albert Hall).

Why you need to know these facts

It is necessary to understand that Britain's power and influence in the Victorian era was founded on its great industrial muscle and wealth. The Great Exhibition was a symbol and celebration of this wealth, and also an expression of the pride the Victorians took in their achievements. It also marked a significant moment in the development of cheap travel for the masses, and of the beginning of excursion travel.

Amazing facts

● Queen Victoria looms large historically but was actually quite small. She was just 1.5 metres (5 feet) tall.
● Paxton's great building eventually gave its name to a south London suburb and to a leading football team.
● Visitors to the Crystal Palace consumed 2 million buns and 1 million bottles of lemonade during the Great Exhibition.

Common misconceptions

Queen Victoria was not amused.

Victoria was a lively child and enjoyed much of her life, even after the death of Albert. She was the most widely travelled monarch ever at the time and spent much of her time on holiday in France and Scotland. She did, however, mourn her beloved Albert for an inordinate length of time and held rather rigid views.

Teaching ideas

● By 1900 the British Empire had grown enormously. Map its extent using coloured pencils (traditionally red was used for the Empire). What has happened to these countries now?

● Choose a Victorian invention (the telephone, the electric lightbulb, trams, and so on) and tell its story. Say what good things have resulted from its invention and what bad things.

● If you were planning a Great Exhibition today on the same themes as in 1851, what would you include in it?

The Railway Age

Subject facts

George Stephenson

James Watt invented the first steam-powered engine in 1788, and Richard Trevithick invented the first locomotive based on Watt's design in 1804. But the real beginning of the railway dates from 1825, when George Stephenson (1781–1848) built a railway to carry coal from Stockton to Darlington. The early railways carried heavy goods and were relatively slow. Robert Stephenson (1803–59), son of George, entered a competition (the Rainhill Trials, in 1829) to build an engine to run from Liverpool to Manchester. His *Rocket* won it with a top speed of around 40km/h (29mph).

Railway expansion

Within a few years, this line was joined to Birmingham and then to London (in 1839). A period of intense development began when railways were built everywhere, sometimes even where they were not economically viable. Investors could not wait to part with their money to aid railway building and the 1840s became a time of 'railway mania'. Gangs of unruly navvies descended on the countryside, causing mayhem and even terror in some areas; cuttings were dug (by hand), tunnels excavated and bridges built. Railway building was a highly visible activity.

By 1850 Britain had over 8000 kilometres (5000 miles) of track, which grew to over 28,000 kilometres (18,000 miles) by the end of the century. This was the end of the stagecoach era and use of canals began to decline, although they continued to be used for heavy goods such as coal.

Isambard Kingdom Brunel

During the period of railway mania, the world's first covered station was built at Temple Meads in Bristol in 1840. This was the brainchild of the astonishingly gifted Victorian engineer, Isambard Kingdom Brunel (1806–59). He was the son of an engineer who was French-born but settled in England in the late 18th century. He liked to be involved in every detail of his designs and was a formidable taskmaster. He would turn his hand to most things, designing trackside buildings for the Great Western Railway, the Clifton Suspension Bridge in Bristol and transatlantic steamships. His ship *The Great Eastern*, built in 1858, remained the world's largest until 1899.

His great railway achievement was the line from London to Bristol, built on a broad gauge. He constructed the Box Tunnel and Paddington Station, and created the railway town of Swindon virtually on a whim. (The small nearby settlement of Swindon was known as 'Old Town' to distinguish it from Brunel's railway village near the canal. The name has stuck to this day.)

Why you need to know these facts

The economic impact of the railways on Britain was enormous. The railways enabled industries (especially coal and steel) to expand and goods to become cheaper. This greatly enhanced the wealth of the nation and employment opportunities. Demand was generated, at home and abroad, for the railway-engineering skills that Britain possessed. Almost no aspect of life was untouched. The ports expanded to cope with increased trade, and the speedy distribution of goods meant that mass production and the standardisation of products increased. People could travel easily to work and this led to suburban expansion. They could also travel easily to the seaside or the Great Exhibition.

With the coming of the railways communication generally improved. Newspapers travelled swiftly, delivery of mail was speeded up and the equipment of war could be transported more readily. By rail, the journey from Liverpool to London took six and a half hours; previously it had taken 24 hours by stagecoach.

Amazing facts

When the Liverpool to Manchester railway opened on 15 September 1830, the Liverpool Member of Parliament, William Huskisson, was struck by Stephenson's *Rocket* and fatally injured, thus becoming the first railway fatality. Stephenson himself drove the train carrying the dying Huskisson to hospital in Manchester, at the then unprecedented speed of 50km/h (36mph).

Common misconceptions

One single person invented the railway.
Like many great inventions, railways were the culmination of discoveries, inventions and bright ideas involving a number of people. Watt, Trevithick and the Stephensons (George and Robert) should each take some credit, as should whoever first thought of using parallel tracks to aid the movement of heavy loads (we don't know who). The invention continues to be refined to this day.

● What would it be like to travel in a train pulled by Stephenson's *Rocket*? Investigate first, then write a newspaper report of an imaginary journey.
● Where have all the railways gone? Examine old Ordnance Survey maps (copies are available in any reference library) to draw the routes of Victorian lines near you that have disappeared. Find out all you can about them.

Factories and industrial towns

Subject facts

The Industrial Revolution

With the invention of machines powered by steam or water, the way in which people worked and lived changed completely. This was the Industrial Revolution and it began in Britain in the late 18th century. By the time Queen Victoria came to the throne, new inventions had created a demand for more power and more factories. Although the first factories were in the country, close to sources of power (they were often called mills), factories needed workers so towns expanded to meet the demand for labour. When there was little work on the land people were forced to seek work in the growing industrial towns. Cotton, imported from America and the British colonies, provided the raw material for textile manufacture, which became Britain's foremost industry. But despite the movement of labour towards the cities, farming and the rural life remained a major part of Britain's make-up.

Working in a factory

Conditions in the new factories were far from healthy. Everything was geared to the rhythm of the machines to maximise production and generally little thought was given to safe or healthy working conditions. Small children as young as seven were commonly employed to work in textile mills, where their size allowed them to crawl amongst the machines to fix broken threads and do other tasks. They could be forced to work for 16 hours a day, six days a week.

Some factory owners were caring and far-sighted, and made enormous efforts to look after their workers, sometimes building homes, schools, churches and hospitals just for them. Quakers George and Richard Cadbury led the way by building the model village of Bournville in Birmingham to house their workers. But mostly factory workers were treated like parts of the machines on which they worked. Children were beaten for minor offences, and workers fined for anything that might slow down production, such as whistling or opening a window. In the engine shop in the Great Western factory in Swindon, the toilets were made so foul that workers avoided using them.

Coal and mining

Factories using steam power generated an enormous demand for coal. Coal was plentiful but it had to be mined, which was a dangerous job. Until 1842, when Shaftesbury's law prohibited it, young children and women worked underground in the mines.

Why you need to know these facts

Factories are with us still today, but during the Victorian period there was a real boom in factory building. It was the factory, mass producing goods often round the clock, that created the wealth upon which Britain's power and prosperity were built.

Amazing facts

● The invention of spinning and weaving machines led to the establishment of huge factories. Swainson and Birley's factory near Preston was one of the biggest, measuring 144.5 metres long, 16.5 metres broad and seven stories high. It had 660 windows and contained a remarkable 32,500 panes of glass.
● Sir Titus Salt (1803–76) owned six factories, campaigned to give working men the vote and funded the building of working men's clubs and chapels. In 1850 he decided to build a new

model industrial village for his textile workers in Bradford. It was called Saltaire. Houses, shops and even a park were built between 1852 and 1872, and still exist today.

Common misconceptions

Farming declined during the Industrial Revolution.
In spite of the growth of factories, agriculture did not decline. There was a boom in farming caused by the demand for food created by a growing population.

Teaching ideas

● Design an advertising campaign against child labour in a factory or a coalmine.
● Many famous shops were founded in Victorian times. Investigate and tell the story of one of them, either a local one or one that is well known nationally, for example Boots or John Lewis.
● Interrogate census returns for a particular year and street. (Census records from 1841 to 1911 are available from the National Archives: **www.nationalarchives.gov.uk**. The website **www.ukcensusonline.com** is also useful for tracing ancestors. Records are only made available after 100 years have passed due to privacy laws.) Re-people a street, finding out as much as possible about individuals who lived there. (You could make a visual presentation along a corridor wall.) Find out all you can about the work that people did.

Schools and childhood

Subject facts

Education pre-1870
Schools did exist when Queen Victoria came to the throne, but they were mainly private grammar schools for the rich and

middle classes, and very expensive boarding and public schools for the aristocracy. Girls from wealthy families might be educated at home, but the poor had very little chance of education. 'Dame schools', run in the homes of local women, provided a very basic education for a small fee, but there was an increasing need for an educated workforce, as well as an educated electorate, and the Victorians realised that this situation could not continue.

Charitable societies, set up by church groups, established monitorial schools which attracted some government grants. For example, the Church of England established one school in rural Wiltshire in 1842 'for the poor of the Parish'. As the government paid out more and more money, it introduced payment by results (in 1862), with set tests in reading, writing and arithmetic (the 'three Rs'), to ensure that its money was not wasted.

The 1870 Education Act

The year 1870 was a turning point. The 1870 Education Act established state schools wherever a church or charity school did not already exist. These were most often in the newly expanding towns and were called 'Board Schools', because the law provided for local authorities to set up 'Boards' to run them. At first, education was neither free nor compulsory, but gradually this situation changed. Some local School Boards (for example, in London) made attendance compulsory for children between the ages of 5 and 13, but the Mundella Act of 1880 eventually made attendance obligatory for all children from 5 to 10. Secondary education as we know it did not arrive until the 20th century.

During the period of payment by results (from 1862), teachers concentrated on the 'three Rs' (and the fourth, registration!) that ensured that the school was financed, so there was a great deal of learning by rote and strict discipline, coupled with attendance medals and rewards for those who came regularly. The abacus, the slate and the cane were key pieces of teaching equipment. Later, the curriculum broadened to include geography, art and creative subjects. Religion was also important.

Childhood

Childhood as we know it is a modern invention. Babies of both sexes up to about the age of five were dressed and treated alike until recent times. After the age of seven they were treated like adults – two children of seven and eleven were hanged as recently as 1708. In Victorian times these attitudes persisted. Child labour was common amongst the poor, where children were expected to contribute to the household as soon as possible. Middle-class children could live happy and secure lives, but we know from Victorian surveys and the writing of people like Charles Dickens that the lot of the poor could be execrable. Parliament had to bring in laws to limit working hours and to encourage education. But in the home, older children had to look after younger ones, do household tasks, clean boots, fetch water, carry coal, darn, sew and cook.

Small children were ideal for task, such as chimney sweeping, and the law was slow in clamping down on such exploitation. Destitute and orphaned children were also a problem and there were many child beggars on the streets, as attested to by the investigative journalist Henry Mayhew. Dr Thomas Barnardo set up the East End Mission in 1867 to care for homeless children. His National Incorporated Association for the Reclamation of Destitute Waif Children became known as Dr Barnardo's Homes.

Why you need to know these facts

Education increased in importance as more and more people were given the vote. The Victorians realised that they must 'educate their masters'. Thus began the state education system that we have today, and to understand it you need to know how it evolved.

Amazing facts

- Out of 17,614 elementary schools in 1880, only 3443 were Board Schools. The rest were voluntary schools run by the church or charities.
- By the end of the 19th century, illiteracy, as measured from Parish Registers, had almost been eliminated. The figure for both sexes was approximately the same: 97 per cent literate.

Common misconceptions

Victorian education was harsh and narrow.
Indeed, it tended to be under the Revised Code (from 1862).
But towards the end of the century, with the abolition of the
Code, things began to change. There is evidence of various
enlightened individuals who used the locality as a teaching
resource and who realised the value of encouragement as well as
punishment and of first-hand experience as well as rote learning.

Teaching ideas

● Compare 'then and now' using Victorian buildings, for
example Victorian school/modern school; Victorian concert hall/
modern concert hall. Identify and describe the main differences
and similarities.
● Investigate evidence from a Victorian School log book. If you
do not have one in school, your local record office should be
able to help. Analyse entries for a year under different headings
such as: discipline, buildings, holidays, the inspectors and the
curriculum. Compare with today.
● Create a Victorian trail around your school/village/town.
You could make a guide book or map using photographs.
● Practise some Victorian domestic tasks such as carpet beating,
washing by hand, using a feather duster. Try cooking a Victorian
dish (check a copy of *Mrs Beeton*).
● Have a Victorian school day. Research the topic first to make it
as authentic as possible – see the resources section at the end of
this chapter for further ideas on reference sources.
● The Victorians built more churches than anyone since the
Normans and created the interior look of churches that mostly
survives to this day. Visit a suitable church and make sketches of
Victorian features. Make a visual guide to the Victorian church.

The Crimean War

Subject facts

The War

The Crimean War (1854–6) was fought on the Crimean peninsula in the Black Sea (see Figure 11). Britain and France, as allies of Turkey, fought (as they saw it) to restrain the expansion of Russia. Fear of the 'Russian Bear' was a recurring theme of 19th century politics. Although the battles took place in the Crimea, it was the more uneventful effect of the fleet blockade of Russia in the Baltic that actually crippled the Russian economy and precipitated the end of the conflict. In the Crimea itself, the overriding impression, as far as the British contribution was concerned, was one of incompetence, bravery and defeat. In fact it was Russia that was crippled, that accepted the Allies' terms, and that took 50 years to recover from the effects of the war.

Figure 11

The origins of the war date back to a petty struggle between France and Russia about who should control certain Christian shrines in Palestine, but it was really about defending the balance of power in Europe, power struggles and the upholding of alliances.

The ghastly battles of Alma, Balaklava and Inkerman, and the destruction of the British army in the winter of 1854–5 through neglect and stupidity, was reported in *The Times* by William Russell (an Irish reporter considered to be amongst the first modern war correspondents). This had a great effect upon public opinion in Britain. For the first time they were able to appreciate the horrors and the mistakes of war. The government came under pressure to remedy matters.

The Russians held on to Sevastopol through the first winter, during which the French and British armies suffered enormously. Cutting supply routes using the Navy eventually brought about the fall of Sevastopol, and from then until peace was struck the exhausted armies did little more than watch each other across the Sea of Azov.

The charge of the Light Brigade took place about five kilometres (three miles) north of Balaklava and illustrates the blunder and bravado that typified the British conduct. Although it was a great disaster, Lord Tennyson focused on the glory and made a virtue out of failure.

In their own words

Half a league, half a league
Half a league onward.
All in the Valley of Death
Rode the six hundred.
'Forward the Light Brigade!
Charge for the guns!' he said:
Into the Valley of Death
Rode the six hundred.

'The Charge of the Light Brigade',
Alfred, Lord Tennyson

Florence Nightingale

Florence Nightingale (1820–1910) was a stubborn, determined and independent woman who, despite opposition, trained as a nurse in Europe. After the Battle of Alma (in 1854), she volunteered to go to the Crimea and organise the nursing of the wounded at Scutari in Istanbul. Using the support of influential friends, she was able to make the journey with 38 nurses. Soon she had 10,000 sick men under her care. She saw that the unsanitary conditions were the cause of the high mortality rate amongst the wounded, and set about remedying the causes.

Because of her romanticised image as 'the Lady with the Lamp', it is often forgotten how formidable her achievements were. She returned to England and set about reforming the training of nurses. Indeed, she spent the rest of her life tackling nursing issues and army sanitary reform, as well as public health in India. She became something of a public institution, living to the ripe old age of 90.

Why you need to know these facts

The Crimean War was the nearest the Victorians came to fighting a major war. It was incredibly expensive, and a drain upon the public purse; it revealed the inadequacies of military organisation and training, and the class-ridden nature of the officer corps. It also started a revolution in both the reporting of war and in provision for the wounded and sick. Florence Nightingale was a critical figure in moving forward reforms in medical services that started in the Crimea but extended well beyond it.

Amazing facts

Florence Nightingale's book, *Notes on Nursing*, was so popular it was reprinted many times.

Common misconceptions

At the Charge of the Light Brigade, 600 soldiers rode into the Valley of Death.
Actually, it was nearer to 700 (*The Times* report at the time mistakenly said 607).

● Research Florence Nightingale. Look for evidence to support what was said about her: interfering, boastful, given to tantrums, unselfish, calm, angelic, extraordinary.

● Find out about Mary Seacole, a nurse of Jamaican-Scottish parentage who also worked in the Crimea and was publicly acclaimed in her lifetime. Compare her life and achievements with those of Florence Nightingale.

The British Empire

Subject facts

For most of the duration of the Empire, the British were never quite sure whether having one was a good thing or not. At the end of the 18th century Britain lost the troublesome American colonies but gained, almost accidentally, vast areas of the sparsely inhabited globe – Canada, Australia and New Zealand. Gradually during the reign of Queen Victoria, Britain extended the territories under its control in India, Africa and the Far East.

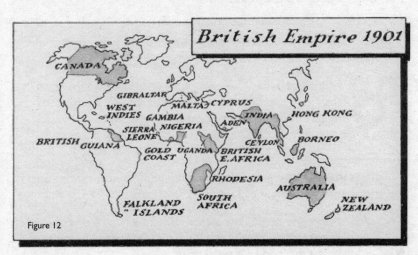

British Empire 1901

CANADA
GIBRALTAR
WEST INDIES   MALTA CYPRUS
GAMBIA
SIERRA LEONE   NIGERIA   ADEN   INDIA   HONG KONG
BRITISH GUIANA
GOLD COAST   UGANDA   BRITISH E. AFRICA   CEYLON   BORNEO
RHODESIA
FALKLAND ISLANDS   SOUTH AFRICA   AUSTRALIA   NEW ZEALAND

Figure 12

The acquisition of territory was sometimes bloodless, sometimes bloody. Exploration of Africa led to new land being annexed, and competition with other European powers gave impetus to empire building in the last decades of the century (see Figure 12 on page 199). Enthusiasm for the Empire waned after the expensive and disastrous Boer War in Africa (1899–1902), and the process of turning colonies into fully independent dominions was accelerated.

The Empire was built on trade. Britain imported raw materials such as cotton and rubber from colonies in the Empire, and exported its manufactured goods such as railway engines and tools back to those same colonies. Britain created the world's most powerful navy to protect its trade routes and the Empire. Historians disagree as to whether the economic advantages of Empire outweighed its cost in the long term; at the time, some 19th-century politicians thought that the Empire was 'a millstone around Britain's neck' (Disraeli, 1852); others were enthusiastic imperialists.

Perhaps the two chief legacies of the Empire (there are numerous others, from the Paisley pattern design to bungalows!) are a multi-ethnic Britain and the use of the English language across the globe. British imperialists gave all sorts of ideas, buildings and institutions to the world, and the Empire gave similar in return, to such an extent that the culture of these islands was changed forever.

Why you need to know these facts

At the end of the 19th century the British had an empire which spanned the globe. It is too large to be ignored and has too much influence on the present to be forgotten.

Amazing facts

Before she died, Queen Victoria ruled over nearly one quarter of the world's population and the British Empire had become the largest the world has ever known.

Teaching ideas

● Investigate the Commonwealth. On an outline map of the world compare the extent of the Commonwealth with the Empire at the end of the 19th century.
● Make a list of all the empires in history that you know about. Write down, in two columns, what you think were the good things and the bad things about them.

Resources

The Victorian era is now beyond living memory, although there are still living people whose grandparents were Victorians and who may be able to recount information told to them about life in the 19th century. But the wonderful thing about teaching the Victorian period is that evidence accessible to children is in plentiful supply. Many children will be being taught in a Victorian school, may live in a Victorian house, or may have walked to school through a Victorian park, past a Victorian postbox or near a Victorian town hall.

Documentary evidence is also extensive so you might consult your local archives or the reference library. Look in your school itself, at school log books, old newspapers, maps, photographs – the list is endless. Talk to people who have taught the topic before, or to local historians and librarians. You haven't got time to start from scratch and there is no harm in 'standing on the shoulders of the mighty'.

Books

There are many books and pamphlets on using written evidence and there has been a huge expansion of helpful material, especially since the advent of the internet has led to more and more people undertaking family history research. The BBC website is a good place to start: **www.bbc.co.uk/familyhistory**. If you want to search for more specific material try **www.familyhistoryshop. co.uk**. Watching something like *Who Do You Think You Are?* (BBC) can give you some ideas, and DVDs of programmes such as the

TV adaptation of *Lark Rise to Candleford* (BBC, 2008–11) will help to put you in a Victorian mood. Extracts from Victorian books, such as *Tom Brown's School Days* by Thomas Hughes (1857) and *Lark Rise to Candleford* by Flora Thompson (1945), can be used selectively with children to serve a similar purpose.

Henry Mayhew's articles, originally published in the mid-19th century, are a powerful source of evidence, if used selectively, and are still available: *London Labour and the London Poor* by Henry Mayhew (Penguin Classics, 1985).

Ordinary Lives a Hundred Years Ago by Carol Adams (Virago, 1982) gives perspectives on the lives of women.

The Butty Boy by Jill Paton-Walsh (Puffin, 1986) is a story set on the canals of late 19th-century Britain. Well-written historical fiction for children such as this can help to set the scene but there are a lot of books out there, so please read before you use as there is a big difference between the good and the bad. Choose books that are first and foremost stories well told; the historical scholarship of the writer should be carried lightly. The acid test is this: Does the book preach at you? Do you feel as if you are being given a history lesson? If that is the feel of the book, then reject it.

Eyewitness: Victorians by Ann Kramer (Dorling Kindersley, 2011) is colourful and informative, using a well-tested format.

My True Story: Dodger! The Story of a Victorian Pickpocket by Jim Eldridge (Scholastic, 2011) and *My Story: Workhouse* by P. Oldfield (Scholastic, 2008) are fictional stories set in real contexts. The series uses short, sometimes clipped sentences, which makes easy reading for juniors at the expense of style. Lots of useful information is imparted.

See also *The Victorians* by Sarah Ridley (Franklin Watts, 2011) and any suitable story by Charles Dickens, an extract taken from *Oliver Twist* that portrays the lives of children in a workhouse perhaps.

Want to know more?

● *The Victorians* by Jeremy Paxman (BBC Books, 2010) – an exploration of the period through paintings.
● *The Victorians* by A. N. Wilson (Arrow, 2003) – a people-focused volume from a well-known writer.

- *Queen Victoria* by Christopher Hibbert (HarperCollins, 2001) – this is a substantial, illustrated paperback and a thorough examination of the person.
- *Life Below Stairs* by Siân Evans (National Trust, 2011) – a well-illustrated source.
- *Empire* by Niall Ferguson (Penguin, 2003) – a thoughtful, well-balanced account of the British Empire from beginning to end.

Chapter II

Britain since 1930

A great deal has happened to Britain since 1930, and there are many people still alive who have lived through the changes. History is, in this case, still part of memory, and there has never been a period of history so comprehensively recorded by electronic and other means. The amount of evidence available is overwhelming. Every historical study is selective (you can never know everything about the past), but in the case of this period, it is particularly important to select and to remain focused on the topics you have chosen to study. Otherwise you will either become confused by the mass of detail, or wander into a study of contemporary affairs.

Most of the changes to the lives of people in Britain since 1930 have been the result, directly or indirectly, of World War II or of technological progress.

Introducing Britain since 1930

Subject facts

Who lives in Britain since 1930?
Since 1930, Britain has become more diverse in its make-up than ever before. World War II truly marked the end of the Empire, and Britain soon rushed to rid itself of the burden of its overseas possessions in the 1950s and 1960s. By no means was all of this transition carried out smoothly or without pain – genocide on the Indian subcontinent is perhaps the best example of this. But Britain found itself impoverished by the War, and searching for an identity and place in the new order of things. It was confused about its role in Europe, and took a long time in deciding whether to join the Common Market.

Timeline	
1933	Peak year for UK registered unemployed – just under 3 million. **Hitler** becomes German chancellor.
1934	30mph (45km/h) speed limit introduced on all roads.
1936	BBC makes its first TV broadcast; King Edward VIII abdicates.
1937	Frank Whittle makes the first jet engine; Nylon manufactured.
1939	First automatic washing machine goes on sale; Germany invades Poland: World War II begins.
1944	Education Act.
1945	Atomic bombs dropped on Japan; end of World War II; National Health Service (NHS) set up.
1946	New Towns Act; Bread rationing, not used during the War, introduced for the first time by a new Labour government.
1948	Bread rationing ends; The Empire Windrush lands the first West Indian immigrants to post-war Britain.
1950	Sainsbury's first self-service store opens in Croydon.
1951	The Festival of Britain opens.
1953	The coronation of Elizabeth II in Westminster Abbey, 2 June; Hillary and Tensing the first to climb Mount Everest; First connections made between smoking and lung cancer.
1955	ITV makes its first broadcast.
1957	The Treaty of Rome establishes the Common Market.
1959	First section of the M1 motorway opened.
1960	17 African colonies become independent in one year.
1961	Yuri Gagarin is the first man in space.
1967	First heart transplant performed by Christian Barnard.
1979	Margaret Thatcher becomes the first woman head of state in the Western World.
1981	The first flip-top laptop computers marketed.
1982	Falklands War.
1998	Good Friday Agreement brings peace to Northern Ireland.
2012	Queen Elizabeth II celebrates her Diamond Jubilee (60 years); Olympic Games held in London.

Emigration to Australia and Canada was one escape for Britons seeking a post-war fresh start and, at the same time, immigrants from the Commonwealth began to change the ethnic mix in Britain irrevocably. Slowly, Britain regained its place as one of the world's leading economies, and also showed a talent for technological innovation. The ability for people to move with comparative ease across continents is now changing the world, not just the ethnic mix in Britain. In modern Britain, you may have your car cleaned by a Polish man, your coffee served by an Australian waitress, your supermarket till operated by a Russian and your bus driven by a Somali.

How do we know about Britain since 1930?

For this particular history topic children have eyewitness evidence and, for the time being, eyewitnesses whom they can interrogate. Although the number of surviving World War II combatants is diminishing rapidly, many people who were young at the time, evacuees for example, are still living today. During their lifetimes rapid advances have been made in the storage and retrieval of information; this has added vastly to the amount of evidence available to the historian. It is worth noting that in spite of this wealth of evidence – artefacts, documents and from eyewitnesses who can say "I know because I was there" – historians still argue over both the facts and their interpretation.

Why you need to know these facts

This period has a critical and immediate impact upon the lives of children in school, especially those who trace their roots to outside Britain. To understand the modern world, you have to study it.

Vocabulary

Adolf Hitler – was the leader (*Fuhrer*) of Germany during the War, and committed suicide when Berlin was captured.
Mussolini – the leader of Italy during World War II; called *Il Duce* ('the leader'). Shot by communist parties at the end of the War.

World War II

Subject facts

This primary history topic presents teachers with a number of alternative points of focus, one of which is the period of World War II. If you choose this as your focus try not to end up with something that is simply a study of military conflict (no one wants to give children nightmares or indeed glamorise and glorify the bombs and bullets side of the most destructive human conflict ever known). However, children (and teachers) do need to know the framework of military events on which the social history hangs, as it had a profound affect on the 1940s and the post-war period. It was a time of great suffering and sacrifice and of terrible acts of inhumanity, as well as of astonishing human bravery and endurance. All educated adults should know these things, but how much you teach your class must be a matter of judgment as to what is appropriate for the age and understanding of the children in your charge.

	Timeline
1939	Britain declares war on Germany on 3 September; Evacuation of children from the cities to country areas begins.
1940	Winston Churchill becomes Prime Minister; British and French troops (337,000) evacuated from Dunkirk after being defeated by the German army in Europe; RAF fights off the Luftwaffe in the Battle of Britain; The bombing of British cities begins (in August) – the Blitz.
1941	Japanese make an unprovoked attack on the American fleet in Pearl Harbor.
1942	Turning point in the land war against Germany: British defeat the German army at El Alamein (North Africa); Russians defeat the Germans at the siege of Stalingrad; Greatest ever defeat of the British Army when Singapore surrenders to the Japanese.
1944	Allied armies land in Normandy (D-Day, 6 June).
1945	VE (Victory in Europe) Day (May); Atomic bombs dropped by the Americans on the Japanese cities of Hiroshima and Nagasaki. VJ (Victory against Japan) Day (August).

The Blitz

Although British servicemen fought in Europe, Africa, Asia and the seas across the globe, the biggest direct impact of the War on the majority of Britons was made by the German bombing raids upon Britain itself during the **Blitz**.

Failure to defeat the RAF in the Battle of Britain in 1940 led the **Luftwaffe** to turn its attention to civilian targets. This was partly to disrupt the industrial infrastructure of the nation, and partly to terrorise the population into submission. The bombing, most of which took place at night, was deadly and horrific, and caused some 60,284 civilian casualties. Of the 45,000 killed, nearly half lived in London, which took the brunt of these attacks. The peak year for casualties was 1940.

The population took shelter where it could find it. Public shelters were built, individuals constructed their own 'Anderson' shelters at home, and thousands of Londoners sought safety in the deep tunnels of the Underground railway system. In spite of its horrific nature, the bombing of civilians during the War has been shown to be largely ineffective. But the Luftwaffe's switch to civilian targets allowed the decimated Royal Air Force (RAF) to recover from the Battle of Britain, and thus the threat of a German invasion was removed.

Evacuation

The evacuation of children to the comparative safety of the countryside proved to be a very significant social event. The intention was to save young lives and to boost the morale of the fighting men by reassuring them that their offspring were safe at home.

Some children were sent by ship to Canada, but for the majority it was a case of internal exile. In the event there were significant unforeseen social effects as a result of thrusting many poor urban children on the rural population. The social classes mixed as never before.

When the German advance into Poland began, the arrangements were made to persuade parents living in the cities to allow their children (most were between the ages of five and fourteen) to make the journey away from the cities and into the countryside.

The first wave of evacuation was a little premature, because nothing much by way of military incident happened at the beginning of the war. Consequently, many civilians miscalculated the extent of the dangers that bombing might bring. Many evacuees returned, and parents were very reluctant to be separated from their children again. This all changed when the Blitz began, but by then, because large numbers of children had started to drift back to the cities, a second wave of evacuation had to begin.

In London, use was made of the Underground network to keep the assembling children away from the mainline stations, and they were taken to suburban stations to board trains to the more remote areas.

The logistical implications were enormous. Posters were displayed making people aware of the disruption to railway services that the evacuation would cause. Teachers, policemen, volunteers from the Women's Royal Volunteer Service (WRVS) and members of the Women's Institute (WI) were involved in escorting, feeding and caring for the travelling children.

What was not expected was the shock that would ensue when city children met country people. On a personal level, the experiences of the evacuees deposited with rural families ranged from loving and caring to the downright cruel but, as a nation, the experience was one that left a lasting impression.

Malnourished, ill-clothed youngsters stirred the consciences of the well-to-do and country people in general, and this led to support, from all classes, for the social and welfare changes that were introduced after the War. Not all the evacuees returned home; this also injected new blood into rural communities and was another impetus to change.

In their own words

Please help me, I can still feel the quick beating of the children's hearts from the bombs dropping under half a mile from the house last Tuesday.

Father's letter pleading for a place
in the country for his children,
Wiltshire Record Office

Rationing

Sharing out essential food and other materials was shown to be a necessity in World War I so the government was quick to introduce it in World War II.

German submarine attacks upon merchant shipping threatened to starve the nation into submission because it was much more dependent upon overseas supplies for its basic needs then than it is now, when farming is so much more intense and productive. The U-boat attacks nearly succeeded and Britain's survival was threatened, but the government stuck to its policy. The diet of children and babies was controlled in a way that it had never been before (or has been since) and was healthy and balanced. No one starved but there were shortages, and a black market in hard-to-obtain goods materialised.

Rationing was administered by the distribution of coupons, and the allowances were varied at different times during the War. The allowance for private fuel was withdrawn completely in 1942. Clothing was rationed (except hats and shoelaces) and this rationing, together with that of various foodstuffs and other domestic commodities, continued until 1954 – nine years after the war had finished.

The role of women and the Land Army

One of the most significant developments brought about by World War II was the change in the role and status of women. Women were deeply involved in doing 'male' jobs in World War I while the men were fighting, but when the war ended so did most of the jobs. Not so this time round: the change in how the role of women was perceived proved to be irrevocable.

Women were essential to the war effort; mainly it was a question of using women to do work at home so that men could be released to do the fighting. The range of work undertaken was much greater than in World War I and there was no resistance to the involvement of women. There was a spirit of 'we are all in this together' that prevailed.

Women flew combat aircraft to and from the factories; they were crucial in the secret code-breaking work at Bletchley Park; they acted as spies; indeed, there was little that they did not do short of actually bearing arms and fighting.

Millions of women entered industry to replace men away at the front and to work on farms – the 'Land Army' was one of the most important roles undertaken. Women effectively took over agricultural production from men. The Women's Land Army was the only civilian service under direct government control, and 30,000 women volunteered for it at the start of the War.

The Home Guard

In the early summer of 1940, when fear of a German invasion had begun to grow, an appeal was issued by Sir Anthony Eden, the Secretary of State for War. Men between the ages of 17 and 65 who had not been conscripted were wanted to form a part-time military force that would take over the role of guarding key installations (such as railways and factories) from the regular army. They would also form an immediate-reaction delaying force should an invasion take place. The force was called the Local Defence Volunteers (LDV), or 'Look, Duck and Vanish' their detractors said. After two months they were renamed the Home Guard and issued with boots.

They were easy to ridicule, especially in their infancy, as they were practically weaponless (broom handles and clubs were part of their 'armoury'), almost totally untrained, and rarely fit for military service. But this gradually changed: initially they were armed with second-rate weapons but later became properly equipped. They manned light anti-aircraft guns and searchlights and lost their 'useless' image. The Home Guard served until December 1944 when they were 'stood down'.

Although the Home Guard would never have been a serious opponent for the German Army it did, nevertheless, play an important role at a time of extreme national danger. Its comic image has been perpetuated in the very successful television series *Dad's Army*.

Why you need to know these facts

World War II was the biggest war in history; its technological and social impact on Britain was enormous. It accelerated Britain's decline as a world power, vastly decreased the nation's wealth, totally undermined the Empire, and brought about irreversible social changes, particularly in relation to women in society. The role of the Commonwealth in the War underpinned the claim of immigrants who wished to live in Britain, and thus kick-started Britain's move towards a multi-ethnic society.

Vocabulary

Barrage balloons – large balloons operated by winches and cables that were used to deter low-flying aircraft, particularly dive-bombers, from attacking particular targets such as factories and ports. During World War II they were often operated by women.

Blackout – a law was passed during the War insisting that all outside lighting was switched off at night, and interior lighting had to be screened from the outside, to deny navigational clues to enemy aircraft.

The Blitz – a shortened version of the German *Blitzkrieg*, meaning 'lightning war'. Used to describe the intense bombing of British cities by the German airforce during World War II.

Doodlebug – the slang name for the powered V1 bomb invented by the Germans in World War II. A terror weapon used with little accuracy against cities. Also called the buzz-bomb.

GIs – General Infantryman or General Issue; slang term for an American serviceman in World War II.

Luftwaffe – the German airforce.

Amazing facts

● Britain was the only country in the War to conscript women, although most of them were not conscripted into the military. By 1943, all women from the age of 18 to 45 were conscripted

to War work unless they had children under 14. War work
could be in the forces (operating **barrage balloons** for example),
the Land Army, or other War-related industry.
● During the Blitz road accidents increased due to the
imposition of a night-time **blackout**. In 1941 there were 9444
deaths caused by traffic accidents. The annual figure today,
with greatly increased levels of traffic, is below 5000.
● Around three million children were evacuated from British cities.
● The blue paper bag used to hold the sugar ration led to that
type of paper being called 'sugar paper' – the name commonly
used for display and art paper in primary schools today.

Common misconceptions

All food was rationed.
It wasn't. Bread, flour, vegetables, fish, cheese, milk and coffee
were never rationed during the War.

Teaching ideas

● Design a poster to encourage parents to evacuate their
children to the country.
● After studying evacuees (perhaps read *Carrie's War* by Nina
Bawden), pretend to be one and write a letter home to mum
describing how you feel. Divide the class into groups and ask
them to think about good experiences and bad.
● Compile a picture guide for RAF pilots to help them identify
German aircraft (a small group activity).
● Using black paper (for silhouettes) and cotton wool
(for smoke and fire), make a large frieze showing the devastation
of the Blitz in London. Use St Paul's as a landmark. You could
add explanatory fact boxes to give information on raids, casualty
figures, dates and so on.
● Build model Anderson shelters using cardboard. Test corrugated
and non-corrugated versions for strength. Write up your results
for D&T.

- Undertake a class project to answer the question 'What did women do in the War?' You could present the answers as a radio programme, an assembly, a visual display or a computer presentation (using PowerPoint® or equivalent).
- Learn and perform some wartime songs. Why are so many of them so weepy?
- Compare the biographies of wartime leaders given in different sources. Compile brief biographies of your own.

The impact of social and technological changes

Subject facts

The Depression

A proportion of the population suffered considerable hardship during the Depression of the early 1930s. This was because the social and economic conditions were such that the people most hit by industrial decline and concomitant unemployment were not financially supported by the state to the extent that they would be today.

The trigger for the Depression was the 'crash' of the American stock market in 1929, the Wall Street Crash. The reasons for this crash were complex and not fully understood, but American consumers reacted by tightening their belts, so America's requirement for imported goods rapidly decreased. Manufacturing nations, like Britain, soon felt the impact of this drop in demand. Belt-tightening became the order of the day and the British government cut spending on just about everything in order to balance the budget, causing suffering, particularly amongst the unemployed. But because the prices of raw materials dropped along with other prices, the standard of living of those people actually in work rose. There was a boom in housebuilding in some areas and the rate of public building rose to 350,000 a year. This meant that the impact of the Depression was not equally distributed across the country.

Steel, coal and shipbuilding – all the old heavy industries – were particularly badly hit. They had already been in a state of decline due to the introduction of alternative power supplies (oil) and a lack of mechanisation and investment that rendered them less competitive against the thrusting new economies of the Far East, Japan and India. Demand for British cotton decreased considerably; the coal industry lagged well behind its European competitors in introducing mechanisation. Even by 1939 there were still 70,000 pit ponies down the mines in Britain and the proportion of mechanically extracted coal had only reached 60 per cent, as against 97 per cent in Germany. A great deal of coal was still hewn painfully, by hand.

The Depression brought down the second Labour government, and a National Government – a coalition with a Conservative majority but led by the Labour leader Ramsay MacDonald – took over. Teachers and other government employees had their pay cut, the dole was cut and began to be means tested, and there was genuine poverty as a result. Photographs of the Jarrow marchers lend credence to the view that workers in the north suffered particularly, as the strain of hardship is visible on the faces of the marchers. Official figures show a peak in unemployment of just below 3 million in 1933, but the figure may have touched 3.75 million in 1932.

In the end, Britain spent its way out of Depression, largely because investment was needed to build up Britain's armed forces for anticipated conflict.

Post-War rebuilding: the start of the National Health Service

Although British aims in World War II were simple and clear – victory against fascism – as the battles progressed and victory became a matter of time, so the feeling grew that we must be fighting for something more than mere victory; social change had to take place. The new post-War Britain had to be better than the Britain of before the War, with its unequal distribution of wealth, dole queues, poverty and under-educated and less-than-healthy masses. The state of many of the evacuees brought this to the forefront of national consciousness – more than any other single event – although the deplorable fitness of many of the recruits into the forces also came as a shock. Pressure for change grew within the serving forces, where educational and political seminars were popular, but it ranged across the social spectrum. Even while the War was being prosecuted the government set up working parties and committees to look into how to improve the nation's education system and its health service.

William Beveridge, previously the successful director of the London School of Economics, chaired a government committee of enquiry into the state of provision in the area of social welfare and health. This committee carried out a widespread investigation and looked at provision from company-run health services to the funding of General Practitioners (GPs). In 1942 it issued a report on *Social Insurance and Allied Services* (the Beveridge Report), which in spite of sounding technical and tedious was nevertheless a seminal document. It turned out to be the catalyst for subsequent legislation that established the welfare state.

Beveridge recommended comprehensive social insurance to pay for a national scheme for health and welfare. In the first general election after the War, a Labour government was elected by a landslide with the expectation and desire for change. It planned for the National Health Service (NHS) to start in 1948, but its birth was subject to considerable pre-natal pain. Doctors had to be bribed to take part, mainly by allowing them to retain some private practice outside the NHS. Every service was intended to be free but the initial rush of overprescription and overuse quickly eroded the free service, although it still remains free in its essential services: a tribute to its creators. The NHS had to deal with a backlog of treatment that had built up over the years because people could not afford proper healthcare before its introduction. Nevertheless, it gradually contributed to improvements in the nation's health which, coupled with growing affluence, led to improvements in living standards and life expectancy during the 1950s and 1960s. The service consequently became a victim of its own success, with more and more demands being placed upon it – a problem that exists to this day. How to meet the needs of an ageing population and how to afford the ever-increasing list of expensive drugs and treatments are problems that are putting a heavy strain on the NHS, and whilst all parties declare their intention to keep treatment free at the point of need, how to do this is the challenge of the 21st century.

The Festival of Britain and the coronation
Two memorable events of the post-War years, which perhaps felt more significant at the time than they seem to be in retrospect, were the Festival of Britain and the coronation.

The Festival (opened in May 1951, the same month as the first *Goon Show*) was conceived as an event that would raise the nation's spirits and bring colour to the years made drab by war and rationing constraints. It was a national letting-down-of-the-hair and was intended to contain echoes of the Great Exhibition of 1851, when there had been a celebration of industrial and technological skill and a peep into the future. Festival of Britain stamps were issued, but the focal event was the South Bank Exhibition, with its Dome of Discovery, Shot Tower, Skylon and Royal Festival Hall. The Millennium Dome and the millennium celebrations are the nearest modern equivalent events. Like these, the Festival had its opponents (most centred on the cost – £11 million) and its problems, but it was, by and large, a success.

Thousands flocked to the South Bank. Parties of schoolchildren came from all over the country, many camping on the outskirts of London in places such as Slough. They were bussed in daily to the Festival to admire the modern machines, cars and other exhibits. Gremlin Grange was a higgledy-piggledy house that poked fun at what was considered to be bad architecture; there was a small zoo and a Festival train (the Far Tottering and Oyster Creek Railway). Down the river the Battersea Funfair was one of the Festival's big successes, although the only lasting aspect of the Festival was the Royal Festival Hall, which remains one of London's premier concert venues.

The coronation of Queen Elizabeth II was a true historical watershed. At the time it was seen as heralding a new 'Elizabethan Age' and there was expectation of a new era of greatness for Britain. In practice, the new age it heralded was the television age. Televisions were bought in their thousands specifically for the purpose of seeing the royal celebrations. The coronation acted as a trigger that set off the nation's love affair with 'the box'. Many people had their first experience of the flickering screen gathered in a neighbour's living room, watching the black and white images of the procession through the streets of London moving on what was, by modern standards, a tiny screen.

The Queen was crowned on 2 June 1953 before a congregation of 8000 in Westminster Abbey. Three quarters of a million people, many from distant parts of the Commonwealth, lined the streets on what turned out to be a wet June day. Souvenirs abounded and schoolchildren were presented with coronation mugs by many local authorities. The Queen was transported in a gilded coach built in 1761, but newly renovated: as a concession to comfort, it was given rubber tyres.

New towns

The urge to rebuild a new and modern Britain to replace the bombed and depressed wastelands created by the ravages of war and the economic depression of the 1930s manifested itself in a concern with planning. The excesses of **ribbon development** were to be curbed, slums would be cleared and brave new worlds would rise in their place. The New Towns Act (1946) created new town development corporations that would extend existing villages and, with their extensive powers, build entirely new communities specially designed to cope with the so-called 'overspill' from the big cities, particularly London.

Within the London commuting area were built Basildon, Crawley, Stevenage and, latterly (1967), the largest: Milton Keynes. Other key new towns were Peterlee, Washington, Newton Aycliffe, Cwmbran, Cumbernauld, Corby, Telford and Skelmersdale. These developments ate up the countryside, and the opposition of the small communities that they destroyed, no matter how vigorously they campaigned, was simply swept aside. To many inhabitants coming from decaying property in inner cities the new homes were paradise. Even so, the new towns suffered from considerable crime and social problems stemming from the turbulence caused by the break-up of established urban communities; many new-town dwellers missed their old tight-knit neighbourhoods.

Population demands have forced recent governments to look afresh at the idea of building complete new towns. In 2007, the government announced a competition to design ten new eco-towns, built with the emphasis on sustainability. How these would tackle the social problems experienced previously is yet to be seen.

Immigration and emigration

Although there is a sense in which Britain has always been a multi-ethnic nation, with a mix of Celts, Irish, Normans, Scandinavians, Huguenots and so on, until the 1950s Britain was essentially a white European country. In 1948, the first

Jamaican immigrants arrived on the ship the *Empire Windrush* (492 passengers and 18 stowaways), and this event marked the beginning of Britain becoming a multi-ethnic country.

Most immigrants claimed right of entry because they were Commonwealth citizens and many of the first contingents were mainly ex-servicemen who had fought in World War II. For political as well as practical reasons, Britain found it hard to refuse entry to those seeking to live here, although there was some opposition from the start. However, their arrival was not considered to be a major issue. (One civil servant is 'credited' with having commented that after one British winter they would all go home.) But chance and need concentrated the immigrants into the poorer and often decaying working-class areas of the inner cities. The accompanying disruption and social strain triggered a debate about immigration controls. Opinion polls taken in 1961 showed that 90 per cent of the public were in favour of them, so in 1962 an Immigration Act introduced a quota system. Alongside this Act were acts against racial discrimination. The Institute of Race Relations was set up in 1958.

In the years following the initial period of immigration, successive British governments have emphasised its positive side. The events of the 1950s initiated the biggest social and cultural change for many centuries and Britain's population now contains several million black Britons. This has enriched the culture and changed Britain's perspective on the world. Britain has also been forced to face up to the moral and religious issues that arise when cultural differences have to be faced. It has also had to struggle with the issue of identity. The British are still divided, for example, on the issue of Europe, and are not always clear which cricket team they should support! (A recent best-selling book by Jeremy Paxman focused entirely on what it is to be 'English' – not a question that it would have been thought difficult to answer in 1939.)

Post-War Britain was also a time of accelerated emigration. There was a great deal of going to (and in many instances coming back from) places such as Canada and Australia. There were many incentives to go, not only the desire to make a fresh start in a new world, but also assisted passage schemes to get the emigrants off to a good start.

The new era of inter-continental mobility plus social changes (the increase in single-parent families, for example), has led to an unpredicted increase in Britain's population. This has meant that the demand for housing has increased enormously, as has the demand for energy and for the basic human needs of food and water. Into this mix go the questions of nationality, sovereignty and ethnic diversity. The 21st century is clearly not going to be without its political headaches.

Technology and social change

Television was the big innovation of the 1950s, but one must not forget that throughout the 1930s and the War years people all over the country were avid listeners to the 'wireless.' *ITMA* (*It's That Man Again*) was as keenly listened to as *EastEnders* is watched today. The world's first regular television service, the BBC, began broadcasting from Alexandra Palace in London in November 1936, but it was not until after the coronation coverage that television programmes really started to develop. In 1958, television licences (8 million) exceeded radio-only licences (6.5 million) for the first time. Radio programmes, such as *Children's Hour*, continued to attract children to the stories of *Toytown* and *Larry the Lamb,* and the mellifluous tones of David Davis enthralled children with the weekly serial, the *Tales of Narnia* or *The Eagle of the Ninth.* Their parents were equally hooked on *Take it From Here, The Billy Cotton Band Show, The Archers* and *The Goon Show. The Third Programme* (now Radio 3) was started in 1946 to accompany *The Home Service* (which was renamed Radio 4 in 1967).

Television's first stars were the newsreaders, people like MacDonald Hobley and Sylvia Peters, and the puppet Muffin the Mule. Television programmes, such as *Newsreel* and *Saturday Night at the London Palladium,* were watched by millions, as was *The Interlude,* a strange, endlessly looping film clip of an activity, such as throwing a pot, inserted when things went wrong with the live broadcasts – which they often did.

Post-War Britain is now long gone; we are in a new world. An adult in the 1950s could not have conceived of carrying a tiny handheld phone and talking with someone on the other side of the world whilst walking down the street, or having a holiday in Thailand or Antarctica, or taking digital images on a tiny camera and transmitting them instantly. Very likely he or she would never have tasted pizza or yoghurt and would never have seen a microwave oven or heard of an electric car. They would laugh at the idea of paying as much as £1.50 (or more) for a litre of petrol (and would not have understood '£1.50' or a litre measure), for around 6p was what they would have paid. But these are just a few examples – if you reflect upon your own life and how it compares with that of your parents and grandparents, you will think of many more, and then perhaps you will come close to comprehending the concept of historical change.

Cinema and records

Cinema-going was at its peak in the 1930s and 1940s, and remained popular through the beginnings of television. Saturday morning pictures were attended by millions of children and could be a fairly riotous occasion. Films such as *High Noon*, *Ben Hur* and *Fantasia* were big hits in the 1940s and 1950s. Changes in the production of records (not 'discs') and record players saw the end of the wind-up players and 78rpm records, and the introduction of 45s and radiograms in the 1950s.

The refrigerator and supermarkets

One of the most influential post-War technological changes was the introduction of the refrigerator to most homes. The technology was not new, but growing affluence and the development of the old war industries to satisfy home domestic consumption generated a demand which industry was able to meet. Patterns of shopping therefore began to change. The daily walk to the shops to fetch fresh food was made unnecessary by the 'fridge' and the growing number of car owners meant that more shopping could be carried in one trip than previously. Small local shops began to close and bigger ones took their place.

The first supermarket opened by Sainsburys was in Croydon in 1950. It was the beginning of a revolution.

The motor car and travel

In 1939 Britain possessed more tarmac road for its area than any other country in the world: over 270,000km (180,000 miles) of road. Its railway network was also extensive – around 30,000km (20,000 miles) of track and 20,000 locomotives – and was reasonably efficient. During the War there was a shift towards rail for the transportation of goods that resulted in a 77 per cent increase in rail traffic and brought the railways close to breaking point by 1945. As part of the Labour government's initiatives when elected in 1945, the railways were nationalised (in 1948), and road haulage and the inland waterways were brought under the control of the British Transport Commission in an attempt to create an integrated transport policy.

But as car ownership increased, an axe was taken to the railway network, which seemed absolutely necessary at the time, although it has been questioned since. Under the 'Beeching Cuts' in 1963, 2000 rural stations were closed. Steam had already had its day and the last steam train was built in 1967.

In 1950 there were 2,307,000 car owners; by 1960 this had risen to 5,650,000. This was the beginning of a trend that still continues. Traffic congestion is not new, for in the 1930s places like Oxford Street virtually ground to a halt even though there were far fewer vehicles in those days. Accidents were at a level far higher than today and resulted in a number of traffic controls. The first driving tests were introduced in 1934 and traffic lights, first seen in 1925, became more widespread.

Travelling began to be a pastime that was no longer the preserve of the rich. In the 1930s it was by bike and foot that many explored the world (these were both growth years for the Youth Hostel Association and years of bitter conflict between ramblers and landowners over access rights). In the post-War years it was by train excursion initially, then the motor car, and the beginnings of foreign travel by air then followed. Britain invented the world's first jet airliner in the 1950s – the De Havilland Comet. The arterial road and the bypass were the invention of the 1930s, and the motorway the child of the 1950s and 1960s.

Why you need to know these facts

Britain of the early 21st century – multi-ethnic, sans-Empire, affluent and hi-tech – has its origins in the last century. To understand today, particularly the multi-ethnic nature of Britain and the industrial changes that have taken place, you need to understand these origins.

Vocabulary

Prefab – temporary housing, post-1944, to meet the need caused by bomb damage. Factory pre-constructed and erected on site, 125,000 had been made by 1948.

Ribbon development – housebuilding along narrow strips, typically following main roads running out of towns and cities.

Smog – intense mixture of smoke and fog that choked Britain's industrial cities, especially London, killing many. Led to the Clean Air Act of 1956.

Amazing facts

- Between 6 and 7 million British people became dependent upon the dole during the Depression.
- Wigs, false teeth, glasses and even prescriptions were entirely free when the NHS began.
- The Minister for Town and Country Planning, Lewis Silkin, had sand put in his petrol tank by opponents to the building of the new town of Stevenage when he visited the area. The station sign was changed to 'Silkingrad'.
- In one of the peak early years for immigration, 1961, 113,000 people arrived in Britain from India, Pakistan and the West Indies.

Common misconceptions

The Festival of Britain took place in London.
In fact, it was a nationwide event with locally initiated processions, fêtes and street concerts, entertainments and parties all over the country.

Teaching ideas

- Compile a class dictionary (illustrated) of key words associated with social change in this period: the Festival of Britain, smog, new towns, the Jarrow March and the Beeching Axe among others.
- Make large cardboard cut-outs of identifiable groups from the period. Research carefully groups such as spivs, teddy boys, mods, rockers, mini-skirted swingers from the 1960s. Write descriptions saying who, when and even why.
- On an outline map of the world, show the flow of post-War immigration and emigration.
- Who were the pop stars grandma and grandad enjoyed? Make a presentation based on interviews and recordings.
- Have a debate about the advantages and disadvantages of reopening old railway lines. Alternatively, do a similar exercise on the value (or not) of the building of motorways.
- If you had a Festival of Britain today, what would you have in it? Devise a programme for the event.
- Watch a film made in the period. Divide the children into groups to note particular social differences from today. Look at dress, transport, hairstyles, shops, interior decoration and design and so on.
- Invite outside speakers to tell the children how they enjoyed themselves 'in those days' – when they were 11 years old. You could choose someone in their early twenties and someone over 60, for example.
- Make a technology timeline showing the main innovations since 1930.

Resources

The sheer quantity of material can make it difficult to cope but, on the other hand, you have plenty to choose from. Don't miss what is readily to hand, particularly people (the school caretaker who was an evacuee, great grandpa who fought in the Army and so on). There will be local evidence to hand as well: a War memorial in the park; an air-raid shelter preserved as a museum; homes and buildings (particularly from the 1930s); a loft full of 1950s toys and redundant domestic equipment. Get the children involved in searches for evidence.

The documentary and visual evidence is vast. There are some wonderful collections of photographs, documents and newspaper extracts available, so a little time searching the internet will be time well spent. The Imperial War Museum and its branches, such as Duxford Airfield and the Churchill War Rooms, offers support to teachers and, of course, excellent museum collections: **www. iwm.org.uk/learning**. The London Transport Museum has a lot to offer on 1930s transport (**www.ltmuseum.co.uk**) and there are similar collections elsewhere (in Coventry, for example). Smaller local museums often try very hard to help teachers tackle specific curriculum projects; the Milestones Museum in Hampshire is a good example: **www.hants.gov.uk/milestones/schools**.

Do not forget that you can use music to impart the feel of the period. Recordings from every decade are still being sold and historic recordings – by, say, Al Jolson, Vera Lynn, Elvis Presley – are easy to come by. Consider not only collections of popular songs but also music inspired by the period. Piano music can be invaluable if you are a pianist or know one who will play for the class; sentimental 1940s songs are a surprising hit with children. It is also worth checking with your local newspaper office to see what they have in their archives. Your local library will probably be able to help. Look for:

● *Union Jack: A Scrapbook – British Forces Newspapers 1939–1945* (HMSO, 1989).
● *London at War The Hulton-Deutsch Collection* (Quoin Publishing, 1989) – a wonderful collection of photographs.
● *The Home Front: Documents Relating to Life in Britain, 1939–1945* (Imperial War Museum, 1987).

- *Ration Book Recipes: Some Food Facts 1939–1954* by G. Corbishley (English Heritage, 1990).
- *The Day They Took the Children* by B. Wicks (Bloomsbury, 1989) – contains personal memories of evacuees.
- *The Best of Times* by Alison Pressley (Michael O'Mara Books, 1999) – plenty of oral evidence and pictures of the fifties.
- *I'll Be Seeing You* (EMI) – a collection of World War II songs.

Books

The events of the mid-20th century have produced a rich harvest of children's historical fiction and the list continues to grow. Do check that you are comfortable with the text before reading to the children, or you may have parental complaints to deal with (Robert Westall's books often contain swearing!). A few to consider are:

- *Carrie's War* by N. Bawden (Penguin, 1974) – a touching tale about evacuees.
- *Goodnight Mr Tom* by Michelle Magorian (Puffin, 2003) – a well-loved weepy about the evacuation of a deprived child to the country; also a TV drama.
- *When the Siren Wailed* by N. Streatfield (HarperCollins, 2000).
- *The Machine Gunners* by R. Westall (Macmillan, 2001) – some language may offend.
- *Blitzcat* by Robert Westall (Macmillan, 2002).
- *The Silver Sword* by I. Serraillier (Red Fox, 2003) – this was originally written and published in 1956, shortly after the date of the events it describes; a classic multi-layered story not to be missed.
- *Rose Blanche* by C. Gallaz (Jonathan Cape, 1985) – a powerful picture book with a difference; it deals with concentration camps (not for the very young).
- *My Story: Blitz* by Vince Cross (Scholastic, 2008) – a fictional offering with factual content.
- *Anne Frank: The Diary of a Young Girl* (Puffin, 2007) – needs no introduction.
- *Anne Frank* by J. Poole and A. Barrett (Red Fox, 2005) – an excellent picture book biography with brilliant, atmospheric illustrations.

Children's reference books come and go all the time but here are a few that are easy to find and will get you started:

- *Eyewitness: World War II* (Dorling Kindersley, 2010) – available with a CD and chart.
- *The Second World War* by Conrad Mason (Usborne Young Reading, 2010).
- *War Boy: A Wartime Childhood* by Michael Foreman (Pavilion, 2006) – illustrated evidence of the time.
- *World War II* by R. G. Grant (Dorling Kindersley in association with the Imperial War Museum, 2008) – if you want to deal with bombs and bullets, this is your book.

Want to know more?
- *Family Britain 1951–1957* by David Kynaston (Bloomsbury, 2010) – detailed and wide-ranging in scope.
- *Hope and Glory: Britain 1900–2000* by Peter Clarke (Penguin, 2004).
- *A 1950s Childhood: From Tin Baths to Bread and Dripping* by Paul Feeney (The History Press, 2009) – a short, lively illustrated account.
- *When British Holidays Were Fun* by T. Tyler (Halsgrove, 2009) – a fascinating, well-illustrated source book.
- *The Thirties: An Intimate History* by Juliet Gardiner (Harper, 2010) – a weighty paperback with lots of photographs.
- *Never Again* by Peter Hennessy (Penguin, 2006) – a very detailed account of the immediate post-War years; highly acclaimed.

Chapter 12

Local history study

Just as every class is a mixed ability class, so every local study is a mixed subject study. And so it should be. Geography, art, design, mathematics and most other subjects are there to be accessed whatever local study you choose to undertake, presenting a perfect opportunity for you to use a cross-curricular approach to learning. If you try resolutely to stick solely to a history theme, even within history you and your children will find a mix of periods, eras and reigns jostling with each other for attention. The past does not come wrapped up in neat single-period packages. Walk down any high street and you will encounter 1950s buildings next to art deco buildings next to 17th century buildings, and so on. Evidence of times past assaults our senses in an eclectic and confusing mix, as if someone was deliberately trying to make a local history study challenging as well as fascinating.

Enough of the warning on the label; this can be daunting but also the most exciting and rewarding of approaches. It can require a substantial amount of preparation and knowledge to make the topic come alive, so what you choose to study is the first important decision you have to make. Given a good focus, the topic can spark interest like no other because it is local, easy to link to the children's experience, and can lead to real, and sometimes even original, historical enquiry.

Why you need to know these facts

Local history provides opportunities for cross-curricular, hands-on history that is close by and can be experienced to some extent. But there is another key reason for undertaking a local study that needs stressing. Following well-mapped national curriculum history pathways can lead schools to overlook the blindingly obvious: the history on their doorstep. It may be some impressive historic monument or site, vernacular architecture, or a local connection with an important historic figure or event, but all of these things can be bypassed when following a prescribed syllabus focused on national or world events. Imagine ignoring Bosworth Field or Richmond Castle if your school was close by. A cotton mill, a coal mine, a railway line, a Norman castle – if these, or similar, sites are close to you they should be considered for study, even if they have long since been taken for granted or considered to be 'stale' or 'old hat'. Remember, almost everything in the world is brand new to young children.

Teaching ideas

How to choose what to do

● The topic must have a *local* dimension, but 'local' can be interpreted fairly broadly, not necessarily as a precise place or within a set number of yards. 'Local' could range from the choice of a wide geographical area down to that of a particular building or person in an area.
● No curriculum straightjacket need apply. The topic could fit into a single period of British history from within or outside the curriculum, or range over several periods.
● Consider to what degree it will help children identify change over a long period of time. Simply comparing 'now' and 'then' will usually take care of this issue.
● Investigate whether you can tie your locality to a significant national event. Is there a local event or development that had national repercussions?
● Apply the same test to people. Is there a significant local individual who affected your locality or events nationally?

Other starting points to consider

The school
Start where you are. This is not for everyone but can be an excellent starting point. Check for old school log books

(maybe in county archives), registers, school newsletters, parish magazines, past pupils, evidence on the building itself and so on. 'Then and now' comparisons are usually quite easy to make and there are many museums that specialise in education topics. Re-enactments are fun and valuable experiences for the children.

Shops and shopping

Look at what has happened in the local high street over a set period of time. Compare grandma's day with today. Look for the legacy of previous shopping practices – ethnic foods, restaurants and so on.

Hospitals and doctors

Start with a 'sick care' map of the area showing hospitals, doctors' surgeries, ambulance stations and clinics. Trace the history of medical provision.

Place names and street names

Walk the streets. Study maps. Who or what are the streets named after? (There is usually logic behind the street names of even a modern estate. Can you tease out the logic behind the choices?) Tell the story of the events that gave names to the streets or places (look, for example, at the Crimean War or industrial sites – 'Brick Kiln Lane').

Local football (or other) club

Depending on the availability of resources, this can be a viable topic. Start with the name of the club and location. This may reveal a lot about local industry and local history. Do not forget to pose specific historical questions to answer. This should not be a version of *Match of the Day*.

Monuments and statues

These can provide excellent starting points. Famous local or national heroes open the door to the study of major historical events. Plaques on the sides of buildings can start the children on a trail of exploration. Check to see if the school has one, just in case.

An historic building

Is the school worthy of study? Perhaps there is a stately home nearby? What about the market or town hall?

A local newspaper

Some local newspapers have quite a long history themselves. Through them you can retell the story of the town over a period of time.

A market history

There are many markets around Britain and many old market towns. Some markets no longer actually exist or have merged into a local fair. Check for possibilities.

Transport and travel

Coaching inns, canals, railway lines, stations, airfields, old trackways, turnpikes, toll gates and so on can all be wonderful starting points.

Hedges and parish boundaries

Specialist knowledge may be needed but the project would involve active research, the use of old maps and plenty of fieldwork. You could carry out a hedge dating exercise.

Bridges, castles and churches

Other major constructions may be equally useful doorways to the past in your locality. If you have an ancient crossing point, a castle or medieval church, then you are fortunate.

A new estate

It may seem a barren land historically but ask the question – *What was it like before?* Until very recently, estate roads usually followed old field boundaries (use maps) because land was sold in field 'parcels'. Check old photographs, the local press and the local museum.

A local traditional event

This could be anything, like the annual handing out of 'buns' at the almshouses in Bedworth, Warwickshire, or the Guy Fawkes celebrations at Lewes in Sussex.

Street furniture

Can be a remarkably rewarding investigation in some places and a good window on how people lived in times past. Check for old postboxes, railings, lamps and lamp-posts, old advertising signs, street signposts, door knockers, foot scrapers, coal holes, manholes, telephone boxes, candle snuffers, shelters, milestones, gates and garage doors, and so on.

A town trail

Devising a town trail can work providing each point on the trail is properly described and interrogated in an historical way.

Industry

If your area offers this topic as a possibility, do consider it. Keep the focus precise (for example, a particular factory rather than industry in general).

Your town at war

The usual caveats about sensitivity apply here – the scars of war are long lasting. Most teachers tend to over-glamorise rather than make this sort of project heavy on blood and thunder. Try to get the balance right. Is there an old airfield nearby that could form the focus for study? See what your area offers.

People

History is about the lives of human beings, so every topic must come back to the lives of people living now and in the past. Focusing on an individual provides another way to do this; a famous poet, writer, engineer, scientist, politician or sportsman can provide doors to the past.

Dealing with whole populations is more tricky. It is much easier to illustrate the lives of Huguenot or Jewish refugees or of foreign settlers – whether they are Vikings or West Indians – by dealing with specific examples. If you can get such examples then this is the recommended approach. You can back up the specific with some general statistical evidence but keep this within the understanding of the children.

Sensitive issues

You may come up against sensitive issues, so tread carefully, but the past does allow us to face up to all sorts of human experiences vicariously. Take a modern issue. *What is it like to be a non-English-speaking Somali in Bristol in 2012? How do they communicate? How do they feel?* Essentially the same questions lose their emotive force when posed in an historic setting. *What was it like for a Saxon farmer when the Normans became his overlords? How did he communicate with the Norman sent to carry out the Domesday Survey when he did not speak Norman French? How did he feel?* (There is an interesting role-play exercise here.)

Handy tip

A walk in the park: a topic route map

To illustrate how a local topic might develop, here is an outline of a line of enquiry that might be undertaken by older juniors. It is a conflation of real activities done by classes of children at various times and in various places, but the topic as a whole has been fabricated as an example.

● The teacher chooses to study the local park with her class after consulting with colleagues, confirming that the topic is viable and checking that resources do exist. The topic fits within school curriculum plans and the children have not undertaken such a project before.

● The teacher chooses the question or questions that the class is going to attempt to answer. *What is the park like today? What was the park like then? What are the key differences between 'now' and 'then'? Can we explain the differences?* ('Then' does not have to be a precise date but should be chosen, partly at least, to fit with the resources available. There may be an obvious reason for choosing a particular time – for example, 'turn of the century'.)

● The class begins the study by discussing the park – which they will of course be familiar with. Descriptions, memories and anecdotes are collected and displayed. (Teachers will decide on how the material from the project is to be assembled and displayed. Almost certainly it will involve a number of different methods – wall displays, project books and so on.)

- The teacher arranges a display of maps ('then' and 'now') for children to examine. A small map extract (that has been enlarged) is given to each child (one of 'then' and one of 'now' if possible).

- A walk in the park is undertaken. (Staffing ratios and any such permission forms are dealt with as necessary.) Notebooks, and as many digital cameras as possible, are taken by the children. At this stage the children are charged mainly with observing and recording.

- A large master sketch map is displayed in the classroom on which the children's findings are recorded. (Place symbols for, or photographs of, park furniture, bandstands, memorials, gates, pathways and so on.)

- A digital photobook of park details is compiled.

- The class discusses its findings and builds up a picture of the park today: its uses, its facilities, its users, its state of repair and maintenance, and so on. Findings might be recorded in writing at this stage. Groups might be assigned to describe and record different aspects of the park today. Interviews could be carried out with park users or parents, for example, to get people's views on the park.

- The class then gathers as much evidence as it can about the park in the past (say, in the 1930s) from people, books, maps, documents and photographs. The teacher puts out a display of resources.

- The class tries to build up a picture of the park as it used to be in the chosen period, asking the same questions about its uses and users as were asked about the park as it is today. *Why is the park where it is? Why is it this shape?* (The teacher checks with the County Archivist for old estate maps.)

- Children are introduced to the term 'legacy'. They consider what they have observed in the park that relates to a time past. (For example, the park's name, memorials and date-stones.)

- At an appropriate time, the class (possibly in small groups) makes a further visit to the park for detailed observation and recording. Art, craft and design activities might be undertaken, such as: pen and ink drawings of buildings or a bandstand; ink washes; oil crayon pictures of flower beds; a composite model of the park.

- The questions originally posed now need to be tackled as a class. This might be done as: a class debate addressing a set question; discussions in groups with whole-class feedback; a class 'lesson'.
- The teacher should consider how the class will finish the project. Is there going to be a specific end-product or products? A class assembly? PowerPoint® presentations? A wall display? A duplicated booklet on the park?
- Follow-up: what should happen to the park in the future? Children could carry out a survey, for example by collating the views of parents, other adults and children. Designs for a new park could be compiled. Ideas could be sent to the local council.

Resources

Once you begin to narrow the choice of topics down you should then ask the question that can (perhaps should?) be decisive. *Have you got, or can you readily obtain, the resources needed to service the study of the topic?* It is no use choosing to launch into a study of, say, Everton Football Club if you have little in the way of books and material to sustain children's interest in the topic. Value the experience of others. What have teachers in your school done before you?

More so than most topics, this one has to be resource-led. If you will excuse a statement of the obvious, the locality is both the topic and the resource. There is always something in the locality on which to hang work of an historical nature; even the most unprepossessing housing estate or rural backwater contains history, although some areas are obviously more challenging than others. Whatever you choose to study, you will need backup and that includes books, pictures and artefacts. If you don't have the material, choose a different topic. There is nothing to be gained from studying a topic that is inadequately resourced.

Everything to hand

In a box, in a cupboard, on shelves or buried in a storeroom, every school should keep a collection of resources to service classes studying locally related topics. You should be able to lay your hands on lots of relevant material without the need to start from scratch every time. This is the kind of resource that a school can build up over time, giving you the chance to build on the expertise and experience of colleagues who have taught similar topics. From my own 'box of delights' the short list below has been constructed. Obviously every 'box' will be different, but this will illustrate the kind of material that can be collected.

- *Photographs (lots of them)*. In local history books; on old postcards brought in by children and old postcards still on sale; newspaper photos from the archives of the local newspaper; photos in personal collections of children, teachers and others (copied for peace of mind); photos in local history collections and photos taken recently.
- *Recordings and written interviews*. The voice of an ex-headmistress talking about her time in the school; an interview carried out by the children with a local farmer talking about changes he has witnessed; an interview with an elderly resident who has, at one time, operated a giant steam hammer in a railway works; an ex-pupil talking about school in the 1930s; an interview with the elderly chairman of the parish council talking about change in the area; the recorded memories of an evacuee.
- *Objects and artefacts*. Domestic appliances; a gramophone; children's games and toys; school slates and reading scheme books; old bus tickets, stamps and coins; old cameras; an old mechanical calculator; an old leather football or tennis racquet; and so on.
- *Documents*. Estate maps; old and new Ordnance Survey maps; school registers; log books; parish registers; wills; shop accounts; old newspapers; and so on.

Books
For books and materials on specific periods you should consult the usual sources, starting with the library. The publications described below offer helpful advice and ideas that may be relevant to the topic of your choice.

The indispensible resource, and reliable starting point, is a good map. The larger the scale the better, but the Ordnance Survey *Explorer* series 1: 25,000 (2.5 inches to the mile) and the *Landranger* series 1: 50,000 (1.25 inches to the mile) are good enough for most purposes: **www.ordnancesurvey.co.uk**.

History in the School Grounds by Jacqui Dean (Southgate, 1999) has lots of interesting teaching suggestions.

Street Furniture by Henry Aaron (Shire Publications) was first published in 1980, but Shire produce many affordable slim paperbacks on a range of topics useful for local studies. For the latest titles see: **www.shirebooks.co.uk**.

A Teacher's Guide to Using School Buildings by Sallie Purkis (English Heritage, 1993) is worth tracking down.

Using the Historic Environment, Practical Ideas and Activities for Teachers (English Heritage, 1996) provides examples of cross-curricular lessons. This, and other titles originally produced by English Heritage, are excellent: **www.english-heritage.org.uk**.

The Ordnance Survey Complete Guide to the Battlefields of Britain by David Smurthwaite (Penguin, 1993) is concise and well-illustrated; see what applies to your area.

Local History in England by W. G. Hoskins (Longman, 1984) is a standard work; masterly, enthusiastic and readable but produced a long time ago. Hoskins worked for some time in Leicester (his local knowledge was used to get an acceptable route for the M1 motorway through Leicestershire), which is now the home of the Centre for English Local History. Check their website for comprehensive lists of sources: **www.le.ac.uk/el**.

Some interesting material may be gleaned from **www. familyhistoryshop.co.uk**.

On specific topics there are, of course, whole libraries of books. On the popular subject of canals, *Canal 250: The Story of Britain's Canals* by A. Burton (History Press, 2011) offers excellent coverage of the topic and fine illustrations. The History Press also publishes many books on the history of specific towns and local topics: **www.thehistorypress.co.uk**.

A book for whetting the appetite, as well as delivering information, is the very personal *David Gentleman's Britain* by David Gentleman (Antique Collectors' Club, 2011). By the famed illustrator and artist, it contains a vast number of excellent coloured drawings of buildings and historic sites, providing some good examples for the children to copy.

The very weighty *Hudson's Historic Houses and Gardens: Castles and Heritage Sites*, 24th edition (Hudson, 2011) is a guidebook and gazetteer to be referred to.

Glossary

Acropolis – centrally located, well-defended area of an Ancient Greek town containing the main religious and civic buildings.

Adolf Hitler – was the leader (*Fuhrer*) of Germany during the War, and committed suicide when Berlin was captured.

Angles – in modern geographical terms, invaders from Germany.

Annul – to cancel, especially the legality of a marriage.

Asgard – the 'heaven' inhabited by the Viking gods, containing Valhalla.

Ballista – small Roman catapult firing iron missiles.

Barrage balloons – large balloons operated by winches and cables that were used to deter low-flying aircraft, particularly dive-bombers, from attacking particular targets such as factories and ports. During World War II, they were often operated by women.

Basilica – a Roman public hall used for administration. With a double row of columns, aisles down the sides and an apse at one end, this set the pattern for Christian churches.

Berserker – a Viking warrior who fought in a wild rage.

Blackout – a law was passed during the War insisting that all outside lighting was switched off at night, and interior lighting had to be screened from the outside, to deny navigational clues to enemy aircraft.

Book of the Dead – in Ancient Egypt, the journey of the spirit in the afterlife was recorded on papyrus known as the 'Book of the Dead'. The journey showed the blissful world of the Egyptian heaven, a land like the Nile, rich in wildlife and food. The Egyptians called it 'The Book of the Coming into Day'.

Buckle – a metal fastening using a pin; remains have been found in grave burials when the material it fastened has rotted. A solid gold buckle was found at Sutton Hoo.

Byrnie – a Viking warrior's protective jerkin, often made of leather

Caldarium – the hottest room in a Roman bath.

Cartouche – groups of Egyptian hieroglyphs contained within an oval shape, indicating a royal or divine name.

Celts – 'Britons' in the context of the Anglo-Saxon invasion of Britain; central and western European tribal peoples in prehistoric and early historic times. Today the term is applied to Irish, Welsh, Scots and Bretons thought of as descendants of these tribes.

Chinampa – the Aztec name for a raised field created in a swampy area for agriculture.

Circumnavigation – to journey around (usually to sail around the world).

City state – a unit of government and settlement (*polis* in Greek). Athens, Sparta and Thebes are examples from Ancient Greece.

Codices – manuscripts of Aztec 'glyph' writing.

Colony – a group of people who have made new homes in a foreign country.

Conquistadores – 'conquerors' in Spanish; the adventurer-soldiers of the 16th-century Spanish Empire.

Danegeld – literally, 'Danish Gold': a bribe, often enormous, paid to the Vikings in order to make them go away. They didn't.

Danelaw – the area of Britain, north-east of a line marked by the A5, where the Vikings were contained at the time of Alfred.

Dark Ages – a name sometimes given to the period between the withdrawal of Roman rule and medieval times. The term refers to the lack of written sources from the period.

Dissolution of the monasteries – the deliberate breaking up of the monasteries and the seizing of their wealth by Henry VIII.

Doodlebug – the slang name for the powered V1 bomb invented by the Germans in World War II. A terror weapon used with little accuracy against cities. Also called the buzz-bomb.

Empire – a collection of countries and peoples ruled by one person or state.

Forum – an open rectangular space that was the centre of business in a Roman town. Also a marketplace.

Frey – Viking god of harvest.

Freya – Viking goddess of love and beauty.

Frigg – queen of the Viking gods; Odin's wife.

Frigidarium – the coldest room in a Roman bath, containing a cold-water pool.

GIs – General Infantryman or General Issue; slang term for an American serviceman in World War II.

Hill fort – a hilltop fortified by ramparts and ditches. Used by the Celts against the Romans.

Hittites – powerful enemies of the Egyptians around 1650BC, their empire centered on modern Turkey and Syria.

Hoplite – a heavily armed infantryman in Ancient Greece.

Hypocaust – the Roman method of providing under-floor heating. Warm air circulated in channels beneath the floor and between walls.

Illumination – colourful and often elaborate illustrations, lettering and borders used to decorate manuscripts.

Irrigation – the provision of water by the use of artificial canals to land lacking in moisture, in order to grow crops.

Jarl – a person in the highest order of Viking society; a lord, warrior and leader.

Jutes – in modern geographical terms, invaders from Jutland.

Kadesh – site in northern Syria of the great battle between Rameses II and the Hittites. Rameses claimed the victory although it was indecisive. The Arabic is *Qadesh* but Kadesh is acceptable and easier to pronounce.

Karl – a person in the middle order of Viking society; perhaps a craftsman or farmer, as well as a warrior.

Kenning – a figure of speech used to give a descriptive, and often poetic, name for something, for example 'whale road' for the sea (from *Beowulf*).

Knörr – a Viking cargo ship.

Longship – the shallow-drafted ships, pointed at both ends, which carried the Vikings on their raids to Britain.

Luftwaffe – the German airforce.

Luxor – the home town of the kings of the Ancient Egyptian New Kingdom from around 1550BC onwards. They built their palaces here and chose to be buried in the rock-cut tombs of the Valley of the Kings (sometimes referred to as Thebes).

m–p

Mussolini – the leader of Italy during World War II; called *Il Duce* ('the leader'). Shot by communist parties at the end of the War.

Nahuatl – the language spoken by the majority of Aztecs.

Natron – a whitish, yellow mineral that occurs in salt lakes. Used by the Ancient Egyptians to dry out fluids in corpses undergoing mummification.

Nilometer – a graduated stone used by the Ancient Egyptians to measure flood levels.

Norseman – another name for a Viking.

Nubians – came from southern Egypt and northern Sudan, an area that became Egyptianised, although Nubians did dominate Egypt in the 8th century BC.

Obsidian – very hard stone (black volcanic glass) used by the Aztecs for cutting and weaponry.

Odin – chief of all the Viking gods, responsible for war and wisdom.

Onager – a giant catapult used by Roman legions to fire a missile over 400 metres – usually ten of these to a legion.

Papyrus – a fleshy plant that used to grow in dense thickets in the Nile marshes. Thin strips were cut from the stem of the reed and laid side by side on flat stones. A second layer was laid at right angles on top. After being beaten with wooden mallets, a surface for writing on was produced.

Parthenon – a temple in the Athenian Acropolis, built in the 5th century BC.

Pharaoh – rulers or kings of Egypt. Pharaohs were so called because they lived in a palace called a great house or *per-ao*.

Picts – in modern geographical terms, invaders from Scotland.

Pochteca – professional merchants in the Aztec markets.

Prefab – temporary housing, post-1944, to meet the need caused by bomb damage. Factory pre-constructed and erected on site, 125,000 had been made by 1948.

Progresses – Elizabeth I journeyed around her kingdom every summer in order to be seen by as many people as possible. These were known as 'progresses'.

Prow – the front of the ship; usually adorned with a fierce dragon's head or similar on Viking war vessels.

Ribbon development – housebuilding along narrow strips, typically following main roads running out of towns and cities.

Rosetta Stone – this provided the key which enabled scholars to read Ancient Egyptian hieroglyphs. It was discovered at Rashid (Rosetta) in the Nile delta in AD 1799. The inscription on the stone was in hieroglyphs, demotic script and Greek. It still took over 20 years to decipher it – an achievement credited to Jean Champollion in 1822.

Rune – a letter in the runic alphabet, made from straight lines; these were used to carve inscriptions, usually on stone tablets.

Saxons – in modern geographical terms, invaders from Germany.

Scabbard – a sheath for a sword.

Scurvy – a disease caused by the lack of Vitamin C, which results in bleeding under the skin, anaemia, and spongy gums. Suffered by sailors on long journeys without fruit or vegetables.

Shabti – also *ushabti*; in Ancient Egypt, models of workers that were buried with mummies and who would spring to life on the command of Osiris to do the work required of the mummified person on their journey through the afterlife.

Sleipnir – the eight-legged horse ridden by the chief of the Viking gods, Odin.

Smog – intense mixture of smoke and fog that choked Britain's industrial cities, especially London, killing many. Led to the Clean Air Act of 1956.

Strigil – a curved scraper used by Romans to clear dirt, sweat and oil from the skin.

Tesserae – small, near-cube-shaped tiles used to make Roman mosaics.

Tetzcoco – the lake and swamp where the Aztec capital Tenochtitlan was built. (Common alternative spelling is 'Texcoco'.)

The Blitz – a shortened version of the German *Blitzkrieg*, meaning 'lightning war'. Used to describe the intense bombing of British cities by the German airforce during World War II.

Thor – Viking god of thunder and justice.

Thrall – a person in the lowest order of Viking society, who would have lived in bondage to a master.

Tlachtli – an Aztec ballgame.

Triremes – Greek galley warships that dominated the Mediterranean well into Roman times; powered by oarsmen in units of three.

Valhalla – the great palace in the Viking warrior's heaven.
Valkyrie – maidens who brought Viking warriors killed in battle to Valhalla.
Vellum – a type of writing parchment made from calfskin.

Wergeld – in Anglo-Saxon times, the price paid for killing a person, a blood price. The more important the person, the higher the price.
Wessex – literally, the land of the West Saxons, ruled over at one time by Alfred and the centre of resistance to the Viking invaders. Centred on the modern southern counties of Wiltshire, Hampshire and Dorset.

Index

Albert (Prince Consort, 1819–61) 184–6
Alexander the Great (356–23BC) 54, 55, 57, 72–3, 74
Alfred the Great (853–99) 111, 112, 119, 121–2, 124, 130
Ancient Egyptians 32–5
    beliefs 41–6
    mummies 34, 42–3
    pharaohs 34, 35, 42–4, 47–50
    pyramids 43–4, 46
    society 35–40
Ancient Greeks 53–8, 64–6, 72–4
    architecture 57, 64
    city-states 68–72
    legacy 56–8
    religion 66–8
    society 59–66
Anglo-Saxon Chronicle 95, 96, 110, 117, 118, 119
Anglo-Saxons 94–7, 100–1, 104, 113–14, 117–18, 121–4
    invasion 98–101

    religion 104–9
    society 102–4
    (see also Alfred the Great (853–99); Arthur, King; Sutton Hoo burial)
Armada, Spanish (1588) 155, 170–1, 174
Arthur, King 110
Athens 68–9, 70
Aztecs 134–9
    cities 146–50
    religion 143–6
    society 139–42
    warfare 150–1

Bede, The Venerable (c.672–735) 95, 107, 109
Beowulf 96, 103
Blitz 207, 208, 212
Boudica (Queen of the Iceni, died AD60) 82–3
British Empire 186, 199–201
Brunel, Isambard Kingdom (1806–59) 188

Cabot, John (1425–1500) 169

ca–gr

Cabot, Sebastian (1474–1557)
169
Canute
(see Cnut)
Caractacus (Celtic leader,
died AD54) 82
childhood 37, 40, 61–2, 140,
193–5
Christianity 89, 104–9, 130,
131, 138
Church of England 154, 160,
164–5
cinema 221
cities, Aztec 146–50
city-states 68–72, 135, 146,
149
clothes
Ancient Egyptians 39–40
Ancient Greeks 61
Tudors 157
Vikings 124–5, 127
Cnut (died 1035) 116, 122–3
conquistadores 137, 139
coronation, Elizabeth II (1953)
217–18
Cortés, Hernán (1485–1547)
135, 136–138, 145, 151
Crimean War (1854–56)
196–9
Crystal Palace 186

Danegeld 116, 118, 121, 122
Danelaw 116, 118, 122

Dark Ages 95
democracy 57, 58, 60, 69, 71
Depression (1930s) 214–25
dissolution of the monasteries
155, 156, 160, 164–5
Drake, Sir Francis (c.1540–
1596) 155, 170, 174

education 61–2, 140, 157,
192–5
Edward VI (1537–53) 155,
160, 169
Egyptians
(see Ancient Egyptians)
Elizabeth I (1533–1603) 155,
157, 160–1, 162, 167–9
Elizabeth II (1926–)
coronation 217–18
Empire, British 186, 199–201
English language 57–8, 64, 72,
94, 117–18, 156, 200
evacuation 208–9, 213
explorers
Tudor 169–74

factories 179, 190–2
Festival of Britain (1951)
216–17, 223

gods
(see religion)
Great Exhibition (1851)
185–6

Great Fire of London (1666)
20–8
(see also Pepys, Samuel)
Greeks
(see Ancient Greeks)
Grey, Lady Jane (1537–54)
163

Hadrian's Wall 78, 83–4
Hawkins, Sir John (1532–
1595) 169–70
Henry Tudor
(see Henry VII)
Henry VII (1457–1509) 155,
159, 163, 169
Henry VIII (1491–1547) 154,
161–3, 169
break with Rome 160, 162,
164–5
wives 161–3
hieroglyphics 39, 40, 141
History Curriculum 5–7, 8–9
holidays 10–13, 182–3, 222
Home Guard 211
homes 14–16
houses 14–16
Ancient Egyptian 37
Ancient Greek 59
Anglo-Saxon 102
Aztec 146
Tudor 158–9
Victorian 181
Viking 124

immigration, post-War 206,
212, 218–20, 224
Industrial Revolution 190
invaders 77–8
(see also Anglo-Saxons;
Romans; Vikings)
inventions 180, 187, 191, 222
(see also factories; railways)

Kadesh (battle, 1285BC) 33,
38, 48
Key Stage 1 topics 8–9

Lindisfarne 108, 116, 118, 119
local history 228–35
London 20–31, 86, 90, 157

Marathon (battle, 490BC) 54,
63, 70
Mary I (1516–58) 155, 160,
163
Mary Queen of Scots (1542–
87) 167
Mary Rose (ship) 155, 165–6
Moctezuma II (Aztec king,
1466–1520) 135, 137, 145,
151
monasteries 107
dissolution 155, 156, 160,
164–5
monks and nuns 106, 109
mosaics 88
mummies 34, 42–3

gr–mu

Index

National Curriculum 5–7, 8–9
National Health Service
  (NHS) 215–16, 223
Navy 122, 160, 165–6, 170–1,
  196, 200
new towns 218
NHS
  (see National Health
  Service)
Nightingale, Florence (1820–
  1910) 197–8
Nile, River 32, 39, 47

Olympic Games 53, 58, 62–3,
  65

Pepys, Samuel (1633–1703)
  20–1, 22, 23, 24, 25, 28–9
pharaohs 35, 42–4, 47–50
place names 94, 100, 101,
  117–18, 119–20, 230
post-1930 Britain 204–6,
  214–24, 225–7
  (see also World War II)
poverty 181–2, 214, 215
Programme of Study for
  History 8–10
Protestant Church 160, 162,
  164–5
pyramids 43–4, 45–6

radio 220
railways 187–90, 221–2

Ralegh, Sir Walter (c.1552–
  1618) 171–2
rationing 210, 213
reformation, Protestant 164–5
refrigerators 221
religion
  Ancient Egyptians 41–4
  Ancient Greeks 66–8
  Anglo-Saxons 104–9
  Aztecs 143–6
  Romans 88–9
  Vikings 129–31
  (see also Christianity)
resources 7
  Ancient Egyptians 51–2
  Ancient Greeks 75–6
  Anglo-Saxons 113–14
  Aztecs 152–3
  Great Fire of London 30–1
  Key Stage 1 16–19
  local history 235–7
  post-1930 Britain 225–7
  Tudors 176–8
  Victorians 201–3
  Vikings 132–3
Roman Empire 78, 80, 81, 90
Romans 79–81
  occupation of Britain 81–5,
  86
  religion 88–9
  society 86–91
runes 103, 125

sagas 117, 125

Salamis (naval battle, 480BC) 54

Saxon kingdoms 98, 99, 118

schools 61–2, 140, 157, 193–5

seafarers, Tudor 169–74

settlers 77–8, 98
(see also Anglo-Saxons; Romans; Vikings)

Shakespeare, William (1564–1616) 175

ships, Viking 126–7

slaves 60, 87, 170

Spanish Armada 155, 170–1, 174

Spanish invasion of Aztec empire 137–8, 151

Sparta 69, 70

St Augustine (died c.604) 105

St Cuthbert (c.634–87) 108

St Hilda (614–80) 108

St Paul's Cathedral (London) 21, 25, 26

Stephenson, George (1781–1848) 187

Stephenson, Robert (1803–59) 187

Sutton Hoo burial 96, 110–11, 112

television 205, 217, 220

Tenochtitlan 135, 137, 146–7

theatre 63–4, 65, 174–6, 183

Thermopylae (battle, 480BC) 54

tlachtli (ballgame) 147–8

trade 111, 170, 173, 200

transport 221–2

travel 11, 149, 182–3, 221–2

Tudor period 154–6
houses 158–9
seafaring 169–74
society 156–9
theatre 174–6
(see also Edward VI; Elizabeth I; Henry VII; Henry VIII; Mary I)

Venerable Bede (c.672–735) 96, 107, 109

Victoria, Queen (1819–1901) 179, 180, 184–7

Victorian Britain 179–80, 187–90, 192, 195, 200–1
society 181–4
(see also British Empire; Crimean War; Great Exhibition; factories; inventions; railways; schools)

Vikings 111, 115–18, 121
beliefs 129–31
invasion and settlement 118–24
ships 126–7
society 124–9

villages, Anglo-Saxon 102–3

we–wr

Welsh 101
wireless 220
women 210–11
    Ancient Egypt 39
    Ancient Greece 60–1, 65,
    71, 73
World War II (1939–45) 11,
    15, 204, 210–11, 207–14
writing
    Ancient Egyptians 36, 39,
    40
    Ancient Greeks 61
    Anglo-Saxons 103
    Aztecs 141
    Romans 91
    Vikings 117, 125

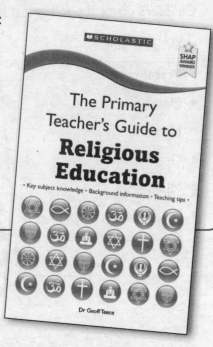

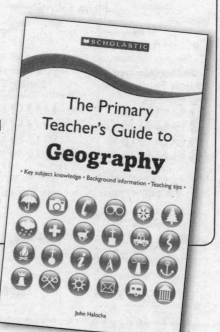

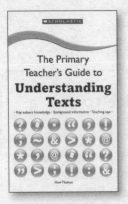

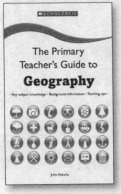
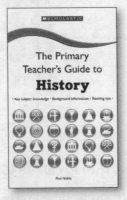
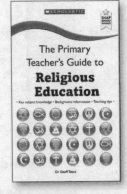